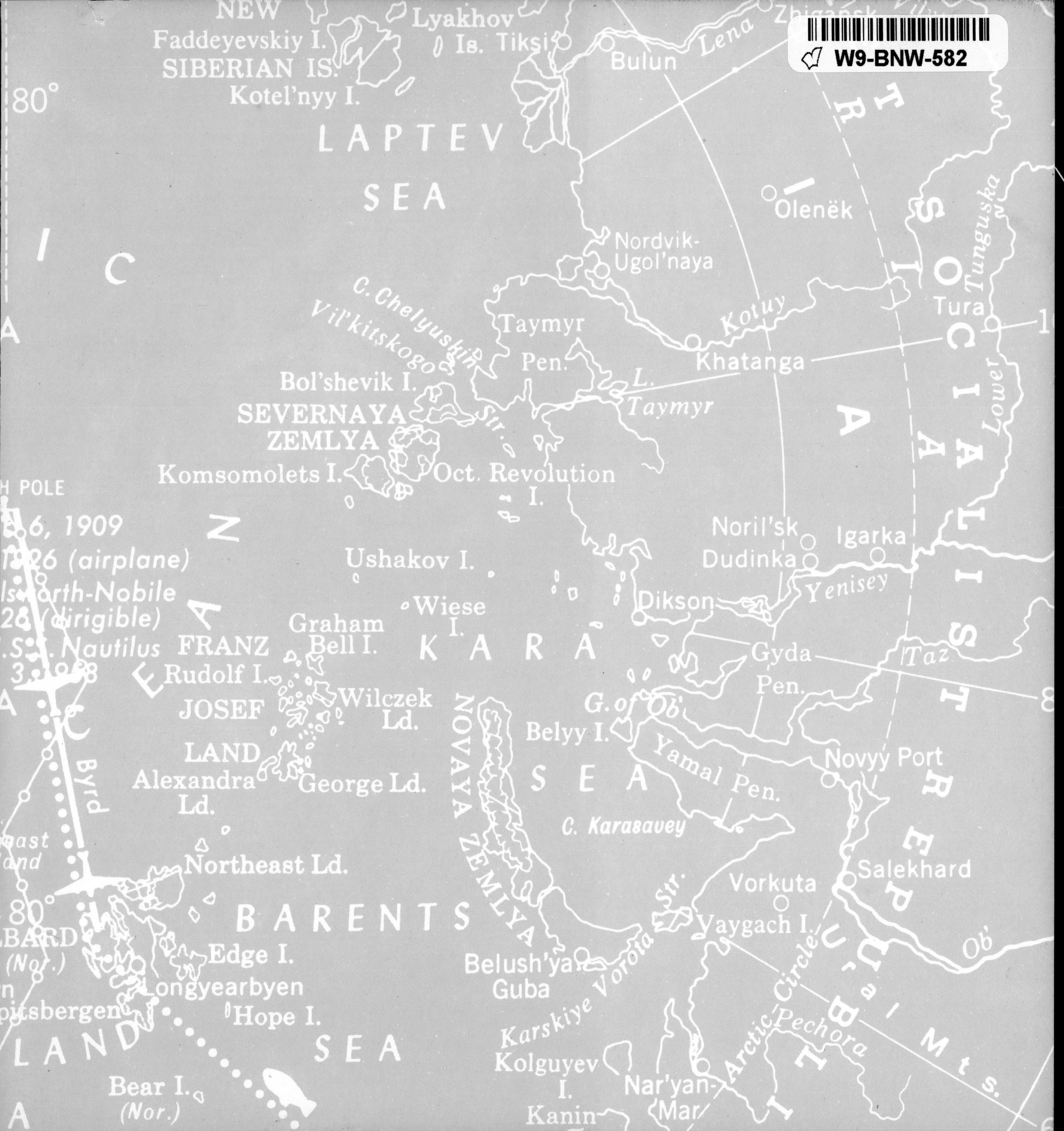

NEW
Faddeyevskiy I.
SIBERIAN IS.
Kotel'nyy I.
Lyakhov Is.
Tiksi
Bulun
Lena
80°
LAPTEV
SEA
Olenëk
Nordvik-Ugol'naya
Kotuy
Tura
Tunguska
Lower
C. Chelyuskin
Vil'kitskogo Str.
Taymyr Pen.
Khatanga
L. Taymyr
Bol'shevik I.
SEVERNAYA ZEMLYA
Komsomolets I.
Oct. Revolution I.
Noril'sk
Igarka
Dudinka
Yenisey
Dikson
Ushakov I.
Wiese I.
Graham Bell I.
FRANZ
Rudolf I.
JOSEF
LAND
Wilczek Ld.
Alexandra Ld.
George Ld.
KARA
SEA
Gyda Pen.
Taz
G. of Ob'
Belyy I.
Yamal Pen.
Novyy Port
NOVAYA ZEMLYA
C. Karasavey
Salekhard
Vorkuta
Northeast Ld.
BARENTS
SEA
Yaygach I.
Edge I.
Belush'ya Guba
Longyearbyen
Hope I.
Karskiye Vorota Str.
Arctic Circle
Pechora
Ob'
Ural Mts.
Kolguyev I.
Nar'yan-Mar
Kanin
Bear I. (Nor.)
Byrd
(Nor.)
H POLE
6, 1909
(airplane)
rth-Nobile
(dirigible)
Nautilus
W9-BNW-582

THE ARCTIC

THE ARCTIC

JOSEPH WALLACE

GALLERY BOOKS
An Imprint of W. H. Smith Publishers Inc.
112 Madison Avenue
New York, New York 10016

A FRIEDMAN GROUP BOOK

Published by GALLERY BOOKS
An imprint of W.H. Smith Publishers, Inc.
112 Madison Avenue
New York, New York 10016

ISBN 0-8317-0391-1

THE ARCTIC
was prepared and produced by
Michael Friedman Publishing Group, Inc.
15 West 26th Street
New York, New York 10010

Art Director: Mary Moriarty
Designer: Devorah Levinrad
Photo Editor: Christopher Bain
Production Manager: Karen L. Greenberg

Typeset by I, CLAVDIA Inc.
Color separations by South Sea International Press Ltd.
Printed and bound in Hong Kong by Leefung-Asco Printers Ltd.

Dedication

For Alice, Julian, and David

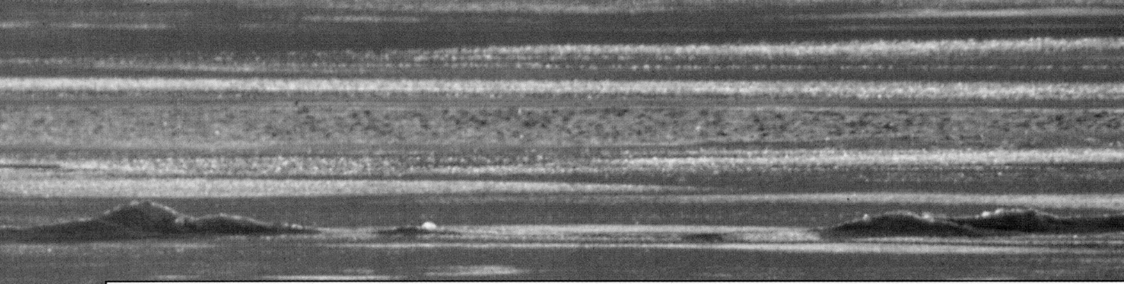

CONTENTS

CHAPTER ONE

THE MOST UNPROMISED LAND

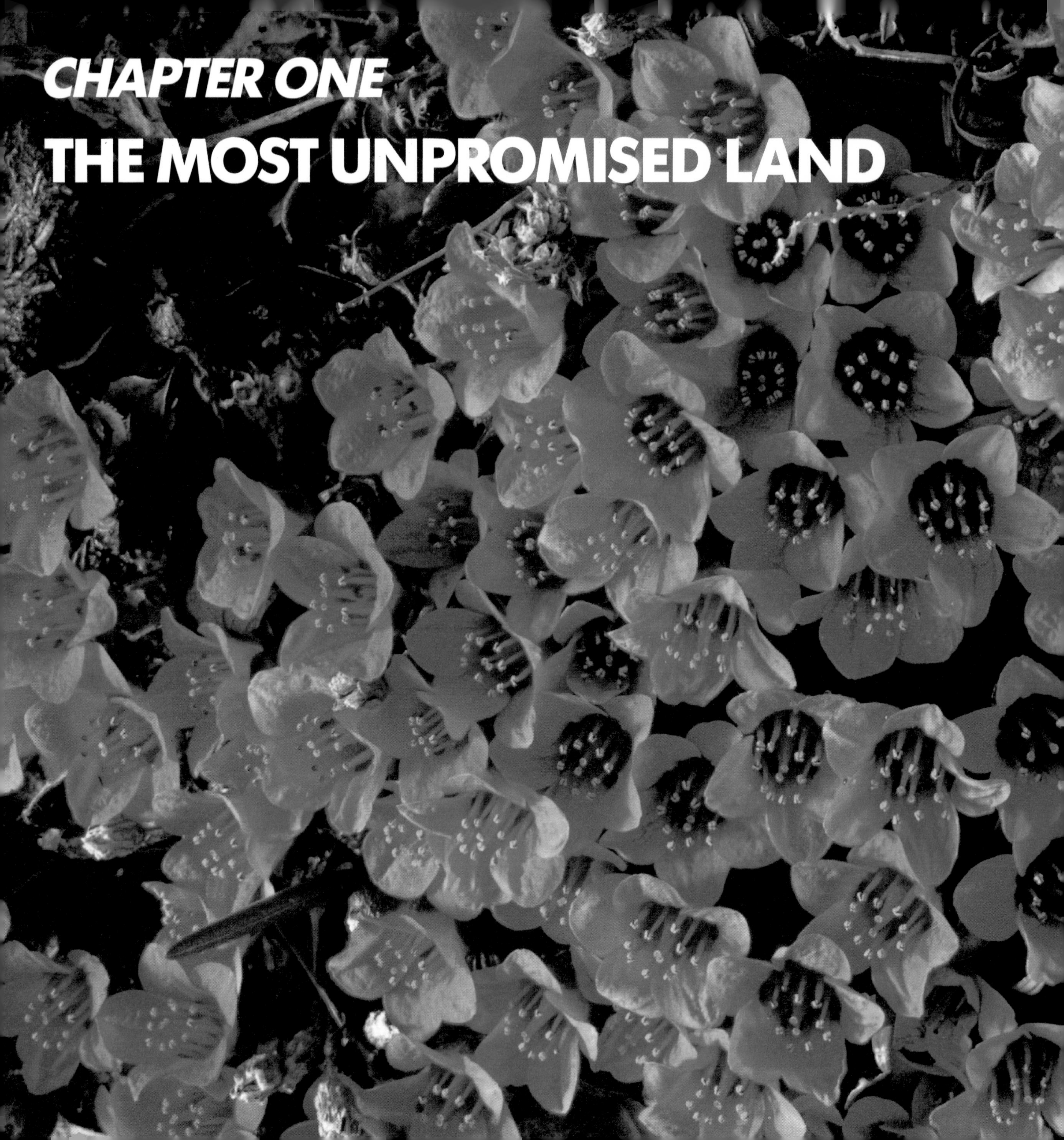

© Pat Morrow/First Light

What do you see when you conjure up an image of the furthermost Arctic? Do you see vast fields of barren, drifting snow? Monstrous icebergs crashing against each other in frigid seas? Explorers buried beneath layers of clothing, their frozen beards gleaming with brittle ice?

If this is what you have imagined, you're right; the Arctic has all of the above in abundance. But that's only part of the picture, a small part. For the Arctic is also a place of dazzling wildflowers blooming during the brief spring and summer. A place where electrical disturbances caused by sunspots create a marvelous nighttime light show called the *aurora borealis* (or *northern lights*). A place whose coldest oceans harbor fascinating animals—ranging from the feared orca whale to the rotund walrus—and whose emptiest, snowiest tundra may hide an unusual mammal, a tiny lemming or a giant polar bear.

For plants, whales, and bears alike—and for the few humans who choose to live there—the Arctic is a demanding home. Months often pass with barely a glimmer of sunshine, months in which the temperature may not rise above freezing. Thick ice may cover the cold waters, depriving fish-

Mt. Tombstone in the Ogilvie Mountains of the Yukon (above) aptly reflects the Arctic winter's frigid desolation. But in spring, the tundra is carpeted with stunning white **Diapensia lapponica** ***and pink*** **Silene acanlis** ***(right), which are only two of the myriad hues the Arctic possesses.***

© Walt Anderson

© Albert Kuhnigk/First Light

© Steven C. Kaufman

eating birds and mammals access to their food. The tortured earth itself may shift under the pressure of melting ice, destroying plants that have survived the bitter winter.

Yet some creatures do live in the coldest reaches of the Arctic. To do so, they must practice innate survival strategies to triumph over the great obstacles posed by their environment. These seemingly overwhelming challenges and the ways that the denizens of the Arctic solve them help explain why the Arctic remains one of the last truly remarkable and mysterious places on earth.

Of all the living things found above the Arctic Circle, none face greater obstacles to survival than plants. In fact, if you were to visit the tundra—the vast, treeless plain that surrounds the North Pole—in winter, you would see an environment seemingly unable to support a single green plant, apparently far too harsh to host a single

The first purple blossoms peek from the hardy buds of the purple saxifrage (far left). The paintbrush's complex, delicate flowers (left) reach for the life-giving rays of the weak northern sun.

flower. "Just what I expected," is what you would probably say.

Yet if you were to return to that same tundra in the summer months you would be shocked to see verdant hillsides, an abundance of brilliant yellow Arctic poppies and purple saxifrage, and once barren fields covered with waving grasses. And, if you're like any other first-time visitor to these parts, you would ask, "How did *that* happen?" The answers, say scientists who are still unlocking the puzzles of Arctic plant life, are both fascinating and surprising.

To truly appreciate the hardiness and adaptability of the Arctic's plants, it's useful to take a closer look at the constant threats to their existence. First and most obvious: The Arctic is cold. All of it suffers temperatures below freezing much of the year, and certain areas are relentlessly frigid for months at a time. Anyone who has ever seen the devastating effects on plant life of a freak ice storm in more temperate regions will quickly realize just how tough the Arctic's plants must be to survive.

Exactly how cold can it get in the Far North? The *average* temperature in Barrow, Alaska, is 10° F (−12.2° C)—and that includes the comparatively warm summer months, which raise the average substantially. Of course, in the winter the temperature can plunge to −50° F (−46° C), remaining at frigid temperatures for months at a time. And that doesn't count the extra chill added by howling winds—which themselves can destroy plants with ease.

The second problem faced by plant life in the Arctic is the lack of light. Of course, this is the area known as the Land of the Midnight Sun, and it is true that for some months each year the sun never truly sets. But even in the warmest months, the heat of the sun is tempered by the extreme angles

At the height of spring, the tundra can resemble an enormous flower garden (left). However, some plants, like the Geum glaciate (below) can bloom at low temperatures, even before the last snow has melted.

Lupines and many other plants have evolved remarkable survival strategies to adapt to the harsh Arctic conditions.

at which it strikes the Arctic region. Plants, which depend on the sun to trigger their food-making process of photosynthesis, simply don't get very filling meals from the weak polar sun. Added to these pitfalls is the fact that the Arctic isn't famous for its sunny weather; even in the height of the summer, dense clouds may fill the sky for days on end. Finally, it is important to remember that the Arctic is also the Land of the Noonday Moon. In other words, although the sun does shine year-round for at least a few hours each day in all but the northernmost regions, months may go by with hardly any light at all.

But say an arctic poppy, a lupine, or a dwarf willow has survived the rigors of an Arctic winter, and now the short spring has begun. Unfortunately, life for these plants is still difficult. Their main challenge is managing to grow, flower, and fruit in a very short time while sitting atop barely defrosted soil that sits above a layer of earth that will never thaw. This layer, well known to anyone who has tried to plant a field in the Arctic, is called *permafrost.*

Permafrost, found across half of Canada and the Soviet Union, more than three-quarters of Alaska, and all of Greenland, is found anywhere that temperatures average below freezing during the course of the year. In temperate zones, the ground freezes during the coldest parts of winter, yet quickly thaws at the first sign of spring. In the frigid Far North, however, the earth may freeze to a depth of thousands of feet, or hundreds of meters, (the record approaches 1 mile [1.609 kilometers]). When the ephemeral spring and summer finally arrive, the warmth of the sun manages to thaw only the topmost layer of soil—ranging from perhaps a dozen feet (about 3.5 meters) at the permafrost's southern limit to less than 12 inches (30.48 centimeters) near the North Pole. The frozen earth below this level has no chance to defrost.

Arctic permafrost poses an array of problems for northern plants. Perhaps most importantly, it forms a wall that prevents roots from digging very deeply into the soil; as powerful as roots can be (and some can burrow through rock), the perpetual wall of ice defeats them. Since trees need to send roots far into the ground, the permafrost sharply limits where they can grow. In fact, the northern treeline isn't dictated by temperature or the fertility of the soil, but the summer-depth of the permafrost.

© Steven C. Kaufman

© Albert Kuhnigk/First Light

Mountain avens (above), bearberry (right), and Arctic cottongrass (far right) impart an ever-changing range of colors and textures in the short spring, summer, and fall. Soon, though, the tundra will once again be covered in a thick layer of ice and snow.

© John Warden

© R. Hamilton Smith

© Robert L. Harrison

During the spring and summer, the permafrost can damage plants in more subtle ways. In temperate regions, rain and water from melted ice seep down into the ground until they are totally absorbed. Here, there simply is not enough thawed soil to absorb the quantity of water resting on the surface. As a result, what was frozen tundra only a few weeks before becomes a morass of sodden earth, messy marshes, and chilly temporary lakes. An unadaptable plant might well drown.

Just as hazardous to plants attempting to anchor themselves into the Arctic's scanty soil is the tendency of the soil itself to drift from place to place. When the rain and standing water come in contact with the permafrost, they aren't absorbed, and so they tend to form vast underwater streams. These streams tend to slide down even the most microscopic hill, carrying the soil with them. The resulting constant—if slow—movement of the earth can twist and shred even the strongest roots.

Yet, as any summertime visitor to the tundra can attest, the foliage that carpets the Arctic during the brief growing season *has* adapted to the vagaries of the region's weather, its lack of light, and its eternal permafrost. In fact, unlike the often scrubby and scattered plantlife of the desert, the plants of the Far North seem almost brazen in their short but bountiful growing season. They're not just getting by, they're thriving. But how?

That's a question that has been pondered by experts for decades, and some intriguing answers are finally coming to light. Perhaps most importantly, the plants that survive the rigors of the Arctic have managed to turn the harshness and inconsistency of their environment into advantages. Take, for example, the dramatic change of seasons, when the frozen tundra quickly transforms itself in a vast swampland. This sudden springtime flood of water is essential to the survival of the Arctic's plants. Without the permafrost's impermeable barrier, all such surface water would quickly become absorbed; amazingly, most plants would soon die of thirst. As meteorologists tell us, this is because, despite its snowy appearance, the Arctic is actually a desert—as dry, in fact, as the great Mojave Desert in the southwestern United States. An average of less than 8 inches (20.32 centimeters) of precipitation fall on the tundra each year, with some areas receiving as little as 1 inch (2.54 centimeters). By

The dandelion-like seedheads of Arctic cottongrass seem hopelessly fragile against an encroaching field of snow. Yet they, like so many other species, thrive in these unlikely conditions.

© Robert L. Harrison

comparison, dozens of inches (a meter or more) of rain fall annually in most temperate regions, while hundreds of inches (several dozen meters) douse much of the tropics.

The Arctic only looks wet because it is so cold. That is, almost every bit of rain or snow that falls is frozen; very little evaporates. As a result, the endless, flat tundra and snow-covered mountains of the Arctic landscape actually support ice and snow that may be decades—or millennia—old. (When Soviet scientists unearth a frozen woolly mammoth from the wastes of Siberia, [as they occasionally do] they must dig the extinct mammal out of the very ice it froze in thirty to forty thousand years ago.)

Thus, without the ancient permafrost prohibiting the meager surface water from draining away, the Arctic tundra might actually resemble a desert—one with little plant or animal life. Despite this seeming stroke of good fortune, however, the region's plants have still had to evolve sophisticated life-support systems to deal with the other adverse conditions.

The most threatening of these conditions are the cold and wind, both of which are fierce and persistent enough to blast all but the hardiest leaves. To fend off these months-long assaults, most Arctic plants grow close to the ground. Hugging the tiny gullies and rocky hillsides that pock the tundra, these plants obtain protection from gale-force winds that might otherwise shred them. Even the dwarf willow, a tree, grows only a few inches—a few centimeters—above the ground in particularly bitter areas, although its branches may stretch horizontally for 20 feet (6.1 meters).

Hugging the ground confers other advantages to plants. For example, there is safety in numbers: When all the plants in an area are small, most will be protected from cold and wind by those around them. Of course, those on the periphery may die, but for the greater good of the whole.

Also, the soil just beneath these low-slung plants is dark; therefore, it absorbs heat from the sun and creates a microclimate far warmer than the air above. Even on the most frigid days, the actual air temperature in the heart

Most northern plants hug the ground, nestling in a warm "microclimate" that protects them from the region's strong, bitter winds.

of a grove of greenery may be well above freezing.

Still, Arctic plants, like all others, depend on the sun. Yet the process of photosynthesis, by which all plants manufacture their food, cannot occur until the air temperature climbs above 40° F (4.4°C). Since this only occurs for a few weeks each year throughout much of the Arctic, northern plants have developed the ability to mature, flower, and fruit far more rapidly than their southern kin.

To produce successful seeds in this forbidding climate requires further complex adaptations. For example, plants that depend on insects for pollination produce large, colorful blossoms, like the bright yellow arctic poppy and the purple saxifrage; these blooms, by their color and scent, are able to summon hungry insects from a long distance. Other plants have developed the ability to pollinate themselves, avoiding the necessity of attracting insects at all. The primitive mosses and lichens require no pollination to reproduce.

Not surprisingly, lasting only a few weeks, the most fertile growing season can not protect any plants from the bitter cold of the months that follow. As a result, many plants become dormant during the winter, while oth-

Lichens (far left) may actually freeze during the long winter months, only to defrost each spring. The moss campion (left) and other flowering plants may depend on "antifreeze" in their sap to keep from freezing.

© R. Hamilton Smith

© Walt Anderson

ers survive only as seeds. Still others have developed a unique antifreeze in their sap, which prevents freezing temperatures from bursting their stems. Mosses and lichens may take the easiest approach: They actually do freeze, but somehow recover and begin to grow once again at the first sign of thaw.

The apparent ease with which plants have developed the ability to withstand the harshness of the arctic climate is a testament to the adaptability and strength of the plant kingdom. It is also a key to understanding all bird and animal life in the Arctic, from the herbivores that feast on these plants to the predators that eat the herbivores. Without the luxuriant growth of plants that carpets the tundra each spring, neither the smallest bird nor the most powerful grizzly bear could survive, and the Arctic would indeed be the barren, lifeless place it often seems.

CHAPTER TWO

MAMMALS OF THE TUNDRA: ICE AGE SURVIVORS

Each year, great herds of caribou (also known as reindeer) wander hundreds of miles across the tundra in search of food (below). This fine bull sheds and regrows his antlers every year (right).

© John Warden

For a land so harsh and seemingly unpopulated, the Arctic tundra harbors a surprising variety of mammals. The cold, challenging north can't begin to compete with the diversity of the tropics, where numerous mammal species may live in a single square mile (2.6 square kilometers) of rain forest.

A dedicated search of the tundra might not turn up a single mammal. But that's because most of these denizens are widely scattered and wary. In a land where food is so sparse and hard to come by, many mammals, such as bear and moose, live solitary lives. They often have vast feeding territories which they must zealously guard against intruders. And even those species, such as caribou, that live in large herds must spend much of the year wandering long distances in search of food.

But a wide range of land mammals have managed to overcome the rigors of unpredictable food supplies, lack of shelter, and devastating cold, and have adapted successfully to life in the Arctic. In fact, at least one northern group of rodents is known for its boom-and-bust population explosions as well as having an undeserved reputation for committing

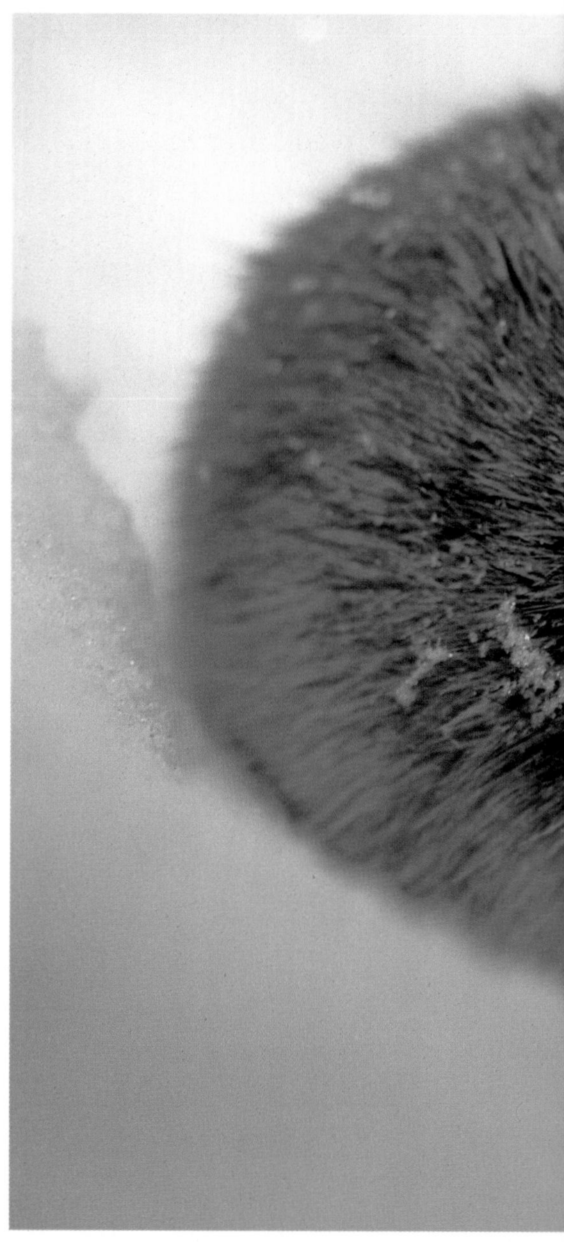

suicide in large numbers. It is, of course, the *lemming*, a breeding machine and a crucial food source for many of the Arctic's larger predators.

Five species of lemmings live in the tundra, digging complex networks of underground tunnels in boggy areas, emerging only to forage for grasses, seeds, and an occasional insect. Amazingly, during the long winters lemmings do not hibernate, as do rodents in warmer climes, but remain in their tunnels or build runways through plants packed under ice and snow. This way they remain sheltered from the cold and surrounded by enough food to last the winter.

When food is plentiful, lemming populations skyrocket. Quickly, the number of animals outweighs the availability of nearby vegetation, and suddenly the lemmings find that they have eaten the cupboard bare. When this happens—every two to five years, experts report—some lemmings starve. But most of the rest begin to migrate in search of richer areas.

These periodic migrations are the source of countless cheery stories of mass lemming "suicide." In their increasingly desperate and wide-ranging search for food, these rodents encounter such natural roadblocks as rivers, lakes, or the ocean itself. Driven by hunger, they do not or cannot turn back—even though lemmings aren't designed for aquatic travel. In these journeys, therefore, many thousands of lemmings drown, starve, or die of exhaustion. They do not, however, purposely commit suicide. Enough always survive to maintain a viable population, which then begins to grow and grow until the next inevitable boom and a new migration.

Lemming population booms have a profound, if temporary, effect on many other Arctic animals. The small rodents make up a major part of the diet of such predators as snowy owls,

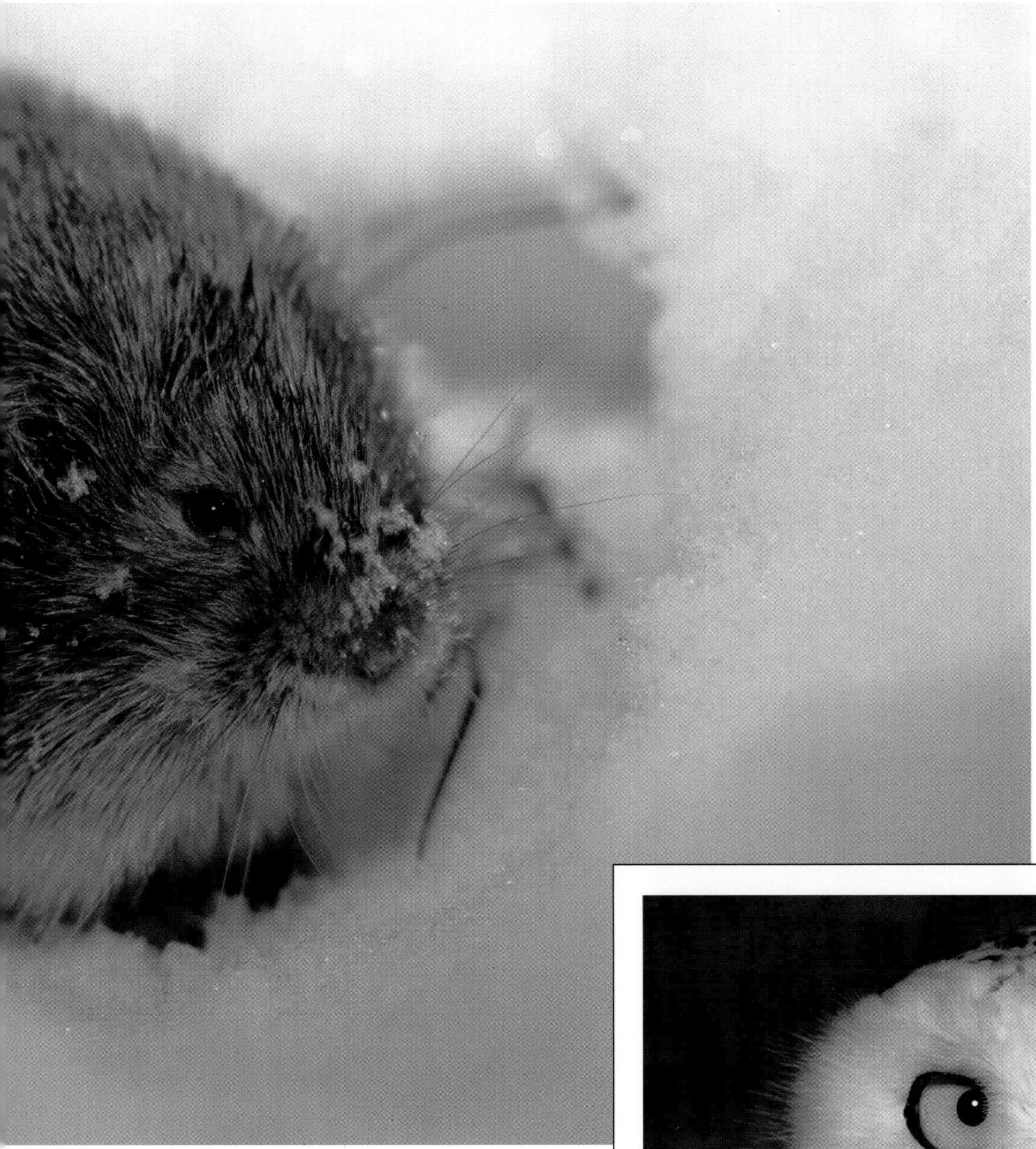

© Dale Johnson/Tom Stack & Assoc.

The abundant lemming (left) is a favorite food of many Arctic predators. The snowy owl (below) will often perch on a tundra hill, watching for a lemming's slightest move, and then swoop in for the kill.

© McAllister of Denver

Arctic foxes, and wolves. In a year of surplus lemmings, these predators may also produce an unusually large number of young, a temporary population boom directly caused by the lemmings. Not until most of the lemmings have starved, been eaten, or left the area do these predator populations return to normal.

One of the most abundant of all northern predators is the Arctic fox, a sleek canine that is one of the most familiar sights of the North American tundra. The mammalian equivalent of the raven, this fox hunts and eats hares, birds, and lemmings, but can also make do with carrion, eggs, and even berries. Wherever there are humans, foxes will scavenge at dumps, often becoming quite tame. But the arctic fox is also willing to follow a polar bear far out onto the frozen ocean surface, lurking about at a safe distance until it has a chance to snatch a morsel of the bear's prey.

© R. Hamilton Smith

© Albert Kuhnigk/First Light

One of the north's most successful opportunists, the Arctic fox will eat lemmings, buds, berries, garbage—nearly anything it comes across. The fox's white coat makes hunting easier during the winter (far left). During the summer, its fur is mostly brown (left).

Both white and blue phases of the Arctic fox exist. In winter, the white phase boasts a thick, dense, pure-white coat that provides superb camouflage against the snowy tundra. The blue phase, found in many of the same areas, has a deep, smoky blue-gray pelt. Both phases turn brownish in the summer.

Far fiercer and more efficient predators are members of the *Mustelidae* family, which includes the familiar skunks and otters. Members of this sharp-eyed and quick-moving family, commonly known as *Mustelidae,* range in size from the tiny and ferocious *least weasel* (weighing in at 4 ounces [113 grams]) to the mysterious, lumbering *wolverine*, which may weigh 50 pounds (22.7 kilograms). Unfortunately, nearly every member of this fascinating family is shy and nocturnal—several years may pass between sightings of some species—although trappers kill thousands every year for their pelts.

The Dall sheep, musk oxen, and moose are just three of the large animals that populate the Arctic. A Dall lamb (below) grazes on Arctic grasses in the spring while a moose cow and calf (far right) pause for a drink. Musk oxen (right) travel the Arctic plains in herds.

© John Warden

© Tom J. Ulrich

© John Warden

Perhaps the most common of all Arctic-dwelling mustelids is the *mink*, which can also be found as far south in North America as the tip of Florida. About 2.5 feet long (76.2 centimeters) and usually weighing about 3 pounds (1.4 kilograms), these lithe animals, with their familiar lustrous brown coats, often live on the banks of well-vegetated streams and ponds of the southern Arctic.

Largely nocturnal, mink are skilled hunters, catching fish, hares, lemmings, and even insects. They are agile both on land, where they move with a distinctive humpbacked lope, and underwater where they can swim for more than 40 feet (12.2 meters) without taking a breath. They also breed successfully enough to withstand extinction by trappers seeking to satisfy the inexorable demand for their valuable coats.

Far less economically important to humans, but just as interesting, is the least weasel, the smallest of its family. Abundant on the far north Arctic slope, the least weasel is, for its size, perhaps the most ferocious hunter of any animal on earth. Those lucky enough to see one usually comment on the aura of intense energy and concentration this mammal projects.

During the brief Arctic summer, the

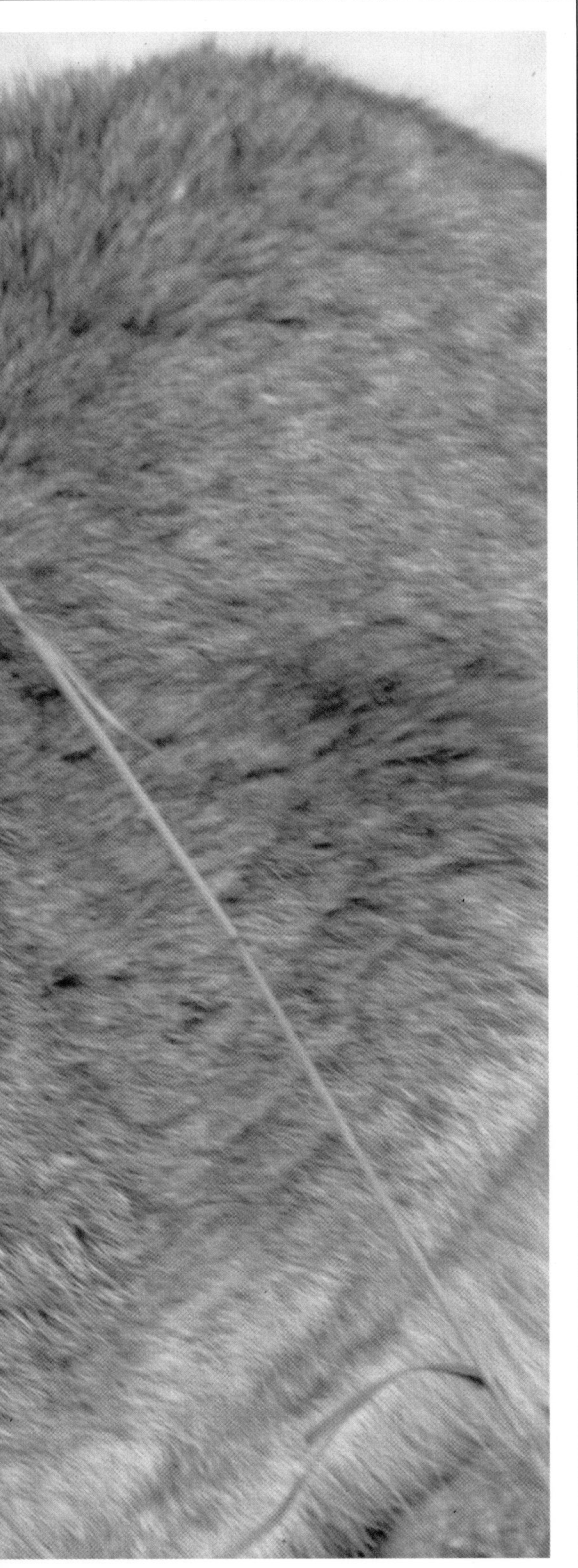

© Rod Allin/Tom Stack & Assoc.

The wary, rarely seen lynx is one of the Far North's most powerful hunters. Its prey can range from hares to trout, and even includes such large animals as the Dall sheep.

least weasel's pelt is dark brown, fading to white on the belly. In winter, like many other animals of the region, it turns white, undoubtedly using its coloration as camouflage as it stalks mice, which it quickly kills with a bite through the skull. In addition, the least weasel hunts birds, insects, and almost any living thing small enough for this diminutive predator to manage.

By far the least known of all North America's mustelids is the *wolverine*, which reaches 4 feet (1.2 meters) in length and can stand 18 inches (45.7 centimeters) high at the shoulder. Too large and shambling to be as efficient a hunter as the weasel or mink, the wolverine is omnivorous, with a taste for carrion. It will, however, kill and eat whatever it can catch (including small deer or mountain goats), as well as settle for berries and seeds.

The *lynx* is a far pickier eater and the Arctic's only wildcat. With its dense, silvery fur and its huge, well-insulated feet—which function as snowshoes—this 30-pound (13.6 kilogram) cat is an impressive sight. However, like so many of the mammals, the lynx is largely nocturnal and rarely seen by visitors to the Arctic.

The population of lynx is closely related to the numbers of snowshoe hare existing at any given time, for it is the cat's principal food. In times of booming hare populations (about once a decade), female lynx may breed before they are a year old and produce litters of three or four kittens. In leaner years, however, the cats may delay breeding and produce only a single cub. Most of the time, the lynx also hunts *Dall sheep* and other animals as well as trout.

Unlike the mink, wolverine, or lynx, the Arctic's hoofed mammals, such as the *moose,* Dall sheep, and *caribou*, are a crucial part of the Arctic scene.

No large mammal is as widespread and abundant in the Far North as the

huge, unpredictable moose. With males reaching nearly a ton (0.907 metric ton) in weight and sporting racks of antlers measuring more than 5 feet (1.5 meters) in width, this largest member of the deer family is a formidable creature. However, except during mating season, when the males can become aggressive and their behavior unpredictable, moose are generally inoffensive animals. You can spot them standing knee-deep in boggy ponds, munching on the tender grasses and other plants that grow there.

Far less common than the moose, the Dall sheep is also more restricted in its preferred habitat. This wild white sheep is found only in the Arctic's jagged, young mountains, leaping nimbly from crag to crag and feeding on grass and shrubs in valley meadows. Such a harsh, unforgiving environment takes its toll on the animals, however. Falls from cliffs, avalanches, and deep snow that hides winter food sources all cause the death of many sheep each year, particularly the young and the aged.

Of all the Arctic's horned mammals, the large deer known as the caribou in the North American Arctic and as the *reindeer* in northern Europe and Asia is possessed with the most wander lust. Each autumn, hundreds of thousands of individuals undertake a migration that may stretch for nearly 1,000 miles (1,600 kilometers), trekking across hilly tundra in search of ages-old winter feeding grounds. Then, with the coming of spring, those that have survived the winter travel the long distance back to the now verdant lakeshores and valleys of the Arctic, where they breed and pass the warmer months.

The caribou is uniquely designed for this wandering life. Its cloven hooves are far more deeply cleft than those of most related animals; with each step, the hooves spread out to form small snowshoes that support the creature's bulk of up to 700 pounds (317.5 kilograms). When the migrating animals must swim across a lake or river, the hooves spread in the same way to act as oars, propelling the caribou easily through the water.

The yearly caribou migration is one of the greatest spectacles of the Far North—but it is also one of the most imperiled. Because the animal requires such a large expanse of land for its survival, even comparatively small environmental changes (such as oil pipelines, railroads, and other signs of civilization) can prevent the caribou from reaching its ancient—

© Tom J. Ulrich

Denizens of the Arctic's treacherous mountain crags, these Dall sheep rams rest and feed in hidden alpine meadows, far from the sight of most observers.

In their remarkable annual migration to their feeding grounds, caribou often must cross hazardous terrain. Many die along the way or as a result of the intrusion of humankind's pipelines and railroads yet, remarkably, the caribou survive.

and essential—feeding grounds. So even though there are more than half a million caribou throughout the world, it is a very vulnerable species.

It's also not the only one whose existence has been threatened by human activities. Perhaps no other animals of the Arctic have captured the public's attention so much as its largest predators: the *wolf* and the *grizzly* and *polar bears.* In recent years, all three have been the focus of intense study and fierce loyalty on the part of animal lovers—as well as irrational fear and hatred on the part of those unfamiliar with their habits. Today, scientists are rushing to learn more about these predators' complex habits, while also seeking to protect them from a multitude of threats ranging from pollution to hunting. What they've found and accomplished makes a fascinating story.

CHAPTER THREE

BEARS AND WOLVES: A PORTRAIT IN BROWN, WHITE, AND SILVER

What is the Arctic traveler's worst nightmare? An eye-to-eye encounter with a grizzly bear, the north's most unpredictable and short-tempered animal (above).

All other tundra inhabitants will go out of their way to avoid the grizzly, even one that seems as peaceful and content as this husky young bear (right).

Everyone knows the grizzly bear—even people who have never seen one. They know that it has slavering jaws, knife-sharp claws, and razorlike teeth. They know that it occasionally attacks humans, dragging campers from their tents, and that it even has been known to eat human flesh. To most people, the grizzly is a living, roaring nightmare, a creature out of a monster movie. Even those who study the great brown bear cannot deny that these horrors are part of the grizzly's story. But this is not the whole story.

The grizzly bear (its name describes its grizzled, grey-brown coat) survives throughout almost all of the Arctic as well as in a few places in western Canada and the United States; it may also be the same species as the brown bear of northern Europe. Wherever it is found, it is perhaps the last truly untamed and untamable northern

© Pat Powell

predator. By contrast, the much smaller black bear (the familiar bear of temperate zones) quickly grows accustomed to humans; even more importantly, it just *seems* less frightening, with its button eyes and shambling manner. Although it, too, warrants keeping a safe distance away from, the black bear can't help looking like a clown.

There is, however, nothing buffoonish about the grizzly bear. Standing up to 9 feet (2.7 meters) high and weighing as much as 1,500 pounds (680 kilograms)—although most are barely half this weight—this humpbacked animal conveys a sense of enormous power and strength. Anyone who has observed this animal in the wild can add that grizzlies are also among the most unpredictable of all animals. A grizzly's mood can swing rapidly from calmness to fury and then back again, often within a few moments. The objects of its momentary rage can be a tree, a small animal, or—in rare cases and usually only when it feels threatened—a human.

When left alone, grizzlies pass the Arctic year like many other northern animals. During the brief spring and summer, they devote most of their time to foraging, eating whatever they can catch. Surprisingly, given their reputation, much of the grizzly's diet is vegetarian. Blueberries, cranberries, grass, and many other plants form the bulk of its diet. In addition, a thousand-pound (453-kilogram) bear will not begrudge a meal supplemented by a 1-ounce (28.35-gram) vole (a common mouselike rodent) or even insects. Those dwelling in coastal areas and along rivers feast on fish, particularly spawning salmon, which they catch by plunging into the water and nabbing them with their needle-sharp teeth.

When the occasion presents itself, however, a grizzly will take on even a full-grown moose or caribou, leaping upon the animal's back after a short charge and dragging it to the ground. More often, however, the bear will attempt to chase an adult moose or other animal away and capture its more easily killed calf. Having eaten its fill of some large animal, a grizzly

will sometimes store the remains out of sight of scavengers by burying them in a temporary cache 6 feet (1.8 meters) deep and more than 10 feet (3 meters) across.

May is mating season for grizzly bears, although cubs aren't born until nine months later, in the cold month of February. The fertilized egg actually lies dormant within the female for months before finally implanting itself in the uterus in October or November. Long before this, the sow bear—having stored an enormous amount of fat from the summer—has found an Arctic wintering site in a grass-lined grove of trees or other sheltered spot.

Here she will spend the long winter sleeping and conserving her energy until the birth of her cubs. At birth, they weigh as little as 8 ounces (226.8 grams), and are blind and hairless. Usually two in number, the cubs will remain with the sow for two or more years before wandering off.

Although the grizzly bear's reputation for attacks on humans is overblown, such confrontations occasionally occur in the Arctic. A female grizzly with cubs is the most dangerous of all, as her protective instinct may overrule the sense of caution that causes most grizzlies to flee at the first sight or scent of a hu-

Although strong enough to kill a moose or caribou, the grizzly primarily feeds on mice, berries, and other vegetation (left). Young bear cubs (below) often engage in "play fighting," good practice for their lives as hunters.

man being. Attacks may occur if the animal feels cornered or if a person approaches too close to a cached kill.

The charge of an enraged grizzly is one of the awe-inspiring sights of the natural world. First, the bear will usually rise onto its hind legs and peer at the person who has surprised it. (A grizzly's sense of sight is relatively weak, but its senses of smell and hearing are acute.) Next, the bear will fall heavily back onto all fours. Its hair will puff out, making it look even more frightening, and—often silently—it will race forward at terrifying speed.

Actually, race isn't the appropriate word. Although moving at more than 30 miles (48 kilometers) an hour, a charging grizzly appears to "bounce" like some malevolent beach ball. According to those who have withstood a charge from an angry grizzly, seeing a puffed-out bear bouncing toward you at great speed leads to a mix of emotions that

Experts have many theories on what to do if you chance upon a wild grizzly. The best advice of all: don't.

includes raw terror and disbelief.

Many of these charges are actually bluffs, in which the bear will veer off and flee before actually reaching its target. Some people have succeeded in chasing off an enraged bear by yelling and cursing and jumping around, thereby apparently denting the grizzly's self-confidence. However, as everyone knows, charging grizzlies sometimes maul and even kill humans. If you are being mauled, experts stress, you must "play dead." Lie as still as possible, no matter what the bear is doing to you. This, however, seems like easier advice to give than to follow.

The gray wolf (below), polar bear (center), and grizzly (far right) all have been mercilessly hunted by humans. If these animals are ever hunted to extinction, the Arctic will lose much of its all-important wildness.

© Ted Levin

© Rod Allin/Tom Stack & Assoc.

© Gerry Ellis/Ellis Wildlife Collection

Few animals on earth are as mysterious as the polar bear, which wanders tirelessly across the remotest tundra and ice pack, far above the Arctic Circle.

That the occasional mauling receives so much publicity may say more about our fear of animals than it does about the grizzly's supposedly bloodthirsty habits. This reputation is far more an invention of tabloid newspapers and hunting magazines than a description of the actual behavior of the bear. More accurately, the grizzly bear is a wild animal, truly wild, in the sense that it considers humans just another part of its world. And this world requires that it hunt and eat meat and protect its food and young. Given space to roam and to find food, and otherwise left alone, the grizzly will remain wild, a refreshing reminder of a time when humans weren't the most dominant creatures on earth.

For most people, the extent of knowledge of the polar bear is confined solely to visits to the zoo. Here, visitors can watch the large, yellowish animals bask in the sun or swim lazily in the mucky water provided for them. Invariably, the animals look affable, grubby, and impressive only because of their great size.

Unfortunately, determining the polar bear's personality from these brief zoo visits is little better than trying to judge the character of a stuffed bear in a museum diorama. Captive

© Tom J. Ulrich

© Leonard Lee Rue III/FPG Intl.

polar bears obscure the truth about these magnificent animals. Only those who have journeyed to the ice cap itself have seen that the polar bear is a remarkably efficient and clever predator, a strong, tireless swimmer, and—even more so than the grizzly—one of the last completely wild and independent animals left on earth.

At 1,200 pounds (544 kilograms) or more (some may reach 1,600 to 1,700 pounds [726 to 771 kilograms]), and 8 feet (2.4 meters) long, the average polar bear is as large as the most enormous grizzly. With its thick legs, padded feet, heavy coat, and small head and ears, it is perfectly adapted for a life spent in the Far North. Its yellow-white coat enables it to blend in nearly flawlessly with the permanent snowfield; only its dark eyes and nose give it away.

The unstable ice cap, cracking and receding in summer, poses no threat to the polar bear. This huge mammal is as comfortable in the water as it is on land, swimming strongly and smoothly in a doglike style. Polar bears often swim a great distance from the nearest solid surface and think nothing of crossing frigid, choppy expanses of water in any season. They are so well insulated—by a thick layer of fat and their luxuriant pelts—that they are as comfortable, if not more so, in wet, subzero conditions.

Most of the polar bear's diet is made up of seals, particularly the ringed seals that are the most common Arctic members of their family. Other foods include walrus, birds, carrion, and even the occasional plant. When tracking their favorite food, however, polar bears utilize a particularly clever hunting technique.

Seals spend much of their time underwater, safe beneath the ice that coats Arctic waters for most of the year. In the autumn, when the ice cap is just beginning to form, seals make sure that a network of small holes remain unfrozen throughout the winter, allowing the animals to periodically return to the surface to breathe. Each seal will have a few breathing holes that it uses repeatedly, a fact that the polar bear soon learns. Choosing one such hole, the bear will

© Robert L. Harrison

The polar bear's whitish coat provides ideal camouflage as it hunts seals on the ice (left). This adaptable bear is equally at home on land and in the frigid Arctic waters (right).

© Ted Levin

wait patiently until the seal surfaces, then swat at it with a powerful paw. It then pulls the stunned or dead seal to the surface of the ice as its next meal.

In warmer months, seals spend more time basking on the ice and are far harder to surprise. At these times, the polar bear must use stealth, sneaking up gradually on its wary prey. The bear's white coat is of great advantage as it travels slowly across the snow, often drawing to within 15 feet (4.5 meters) without being spotted. Some experts report that a hunting polar bear will actually hide its black nose with a paw while stalking a basking seal, but this may just be legend. The polar bear covers the last short distance of the hunt in a sudden dash, during which the seal desperately tries to reach the safety of the water. If this attempt proves unsuccessful, a polar bear will patiently begin the procedure again with another target.

Horror stories of human-bear encounters are less frequent with polar bears than with grizzlies—but not because the great white bear is tamer. Instead, it has even less need for human company; many Arctic polar bears may spend their lives without having close contact with a single human. In fact, when people and

Portraits in the wild. The polar bear's black, expressionless eyes reveal nothing of the powerful hunter within (below). The wolf's eyes (right) are clearer, more expressive—and, to some people, disturbingly similar to human eyes.

© Steven C. Kaufman

bears meet, polar bears can be doubly dangerous because they have not learned to fear humans or their guns.

Despite the fear and distrust that many people display toward grizzly and polar bears, no Arctic-dwelling animal—perhaps no animal on earth—has been more unfairly despised and distrusted than the wolf. From ancient fairy-tales and legends to the hunters and governments that until recently slaughtered them throughout the Arctic, to the never-caught perpetrator who poisoned two tame wolves while in New York City several years ago, wolves have borne the brunt of human loathing and superstition for centuries.

Why this is the case is hard to understand. No other animal so resembles the dog, our most beloved pet. Hunters in Alaska may have a kennel filled with Siberian huskies, yet will despise the wolf, which is so closely related to the dogs that fertile wolfhuskie offspring commonly occur. In addition, there has never been a single reported attack on a human by a healthy wolf (very rarely a wolf afflicted with rabies will attack someone), despite generations of close proximity in the Soviet Union, northern Canada, and elsewhere. Wolves don't eat very much livestock; they tend to survive in relatively unpopulated areas. Wolves are affectionate parents, with a complex social structure not unlike our own.

In fact, wolf family life is among the most interactive and cooperative of that of any animal. As everyone knows, most wolves live in packs of about five or so animals, usually made up of parents, pups, and a few that are unrelated. When the young are born, they are cared for by every member of the pack, especially by their unattached aunts and uncles, who will frequently baby-sit for them.

There is nothing gruesome or even unsavory about these or other details of wolf life. Why then, until barely two decades ago, did Alaska offer a bounty on wolves—an actual reward for killing them? In some cases, the answer is obvious. Hunters, for example, dislike wolves because they believe that the big canines keep down the population of moose and other

© Tom J. Ulrich

The wolf is a nonaggressive animal with a charmingly attentive and affectionate family life. Even so, excessive hunting and misguided predator control techniques cast a shadow on its future.

animals that *they* want to kill.

A good reason is harder to find in the nonhunting human population, but one theory stands out. Wolves, says this theory, are hated because they seem both intelligent and remote from us. Their pale, penetrating eyes and cool demeanor make us nervous—and we hate—and kill—what scares us. True or not, *something* has made us wage war on the wolf.

Luckily, despite these past efforts, the Arctic remains large enough to support an increasing number of people as well as such untamed creatures as the grizzly, polar bear, and wolf. Will we be able to say the same a decade from now? No one can know for sure, but few would deny that the Arctic itself will lose much of its mystery, beauty, and power—the very elements that draw people to it—if these and other animals disappear from this region forever.

CHAPTER FOUR

SEALS AND WALRUSES: LIFE ALONG THE ICE CAP

Consider the advantages of living in the Arctic Ocean. Perhaps most importantly, except on the surface, it never freezes; in fact, even when the air temperature is a bone-crushingly bitter −50° F. (−46° C.), the water remains a relatively balmy 32° F. (0° C.), give or take a few degrees.

You're not convinced? There's also plenty of room—Arctic Alaska, Siberia, and Greenland, are surrounded on all sides by vast expanses of water. Finally, even these cold oceans are filled with food, particularly if you like to eat fish, mollusks, or crabs.

Sound good? In fact, the waters of the Arctic are a haven for seals, walruses, and other marine mammals, among the most interesting, unusual, and little-understood animals left on earth. However, even for these creatures, the ocean presents a wealth of challenges different from any of those faced by land animals.

The biggest challenge facing all Arctic-dwelling mammals (as well as the seabirds that also depend on the oceans for food) is finding open, unfrozen water during the depths of winter, when much of the Arctic

Arctic seas are bitterly cold, and frequently nearly covered with ice (below)—but they are also rich in fish, clams, and other foods for walruses (left) and many other marine animals.

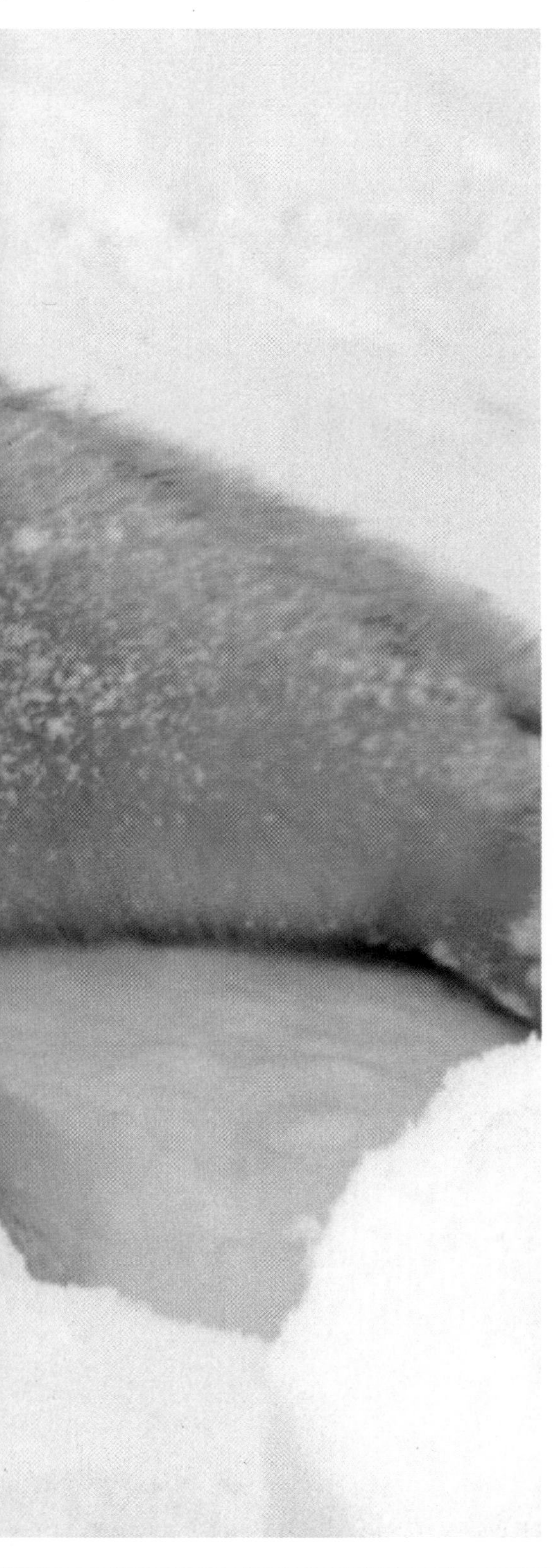

The abundant Arctic harp seal has caused international controversy for the way in which commercial hunters mercilessly club the pups to death for their valuable pelts.

Ocean's surface is covered with ice. Without the remarkable phenomena known as *polynyas*, some of the most fascinating of all Arctic-dwelling creatures would quickly disappear.

Polynyas are large areas of ocean surface, as large as 30,000 square miles (77,700 square kilometers) that never freeze, no matter how cold the air temperature. Native hunters and scientists have long known that these frost-free zones recur every year in the same place, with rare exceptions.

Knowing that such areas exist, however, is not the same as understanding why. In recent years, researchers have finally discovered a simple yet unexpected reason for the polynyas' regular appearance. In these scattered areas, strong winds continually push away surface water, which, being closest to the bone-chilling air, is naturally coldest. Whatever ice has begun to form across the open expanse is soon piled up against nearby thicker ice, while the polynya itself remains unfrozen.

When the near-freezing surface water is pushed aside, it is replaced by slightly warmer water welling up from the ocean depths. These deep-water currents are extremely rich in organic nutrients, the result of the gradual decomposition of marine plants and animals. The nutrients encourage the growth of algae, plankton, and other tiny organisms, which then spurs the population of fish—and a successful food chain is formed. For the murres, seals, walruses, and other creatures that brave the winter Arctic seas, the polynyas provide not only patches of open ocean to swim in, but abundant food as well.

Perhaps the most common mammal found at polynyas and elsewhere in the Far North is the *spotted seal*, a member of the Pinnipedia suborder and a close relative of the more familiar harbor seal. Silvery gray in color, with a rich speckling of dark brown or black spots, the spotted seal can weigh up to 300 pounds (136 kilograms). Like all true seals (as opposed to sea lions), these animals lack external ears, and their hind flippers are not of much use to them on land. For this reason, seals are nearly helpless out of the water, wriggling laboriously like giant slugs when they must move.

Throughout the year, the spotted seal follows the vagaries of the ice pack that constantly advances and recedes across the Arctic's waters. In winter, most congregate far south of the Arctic Circle, at the southernmost fringes of the ice pack. When spring

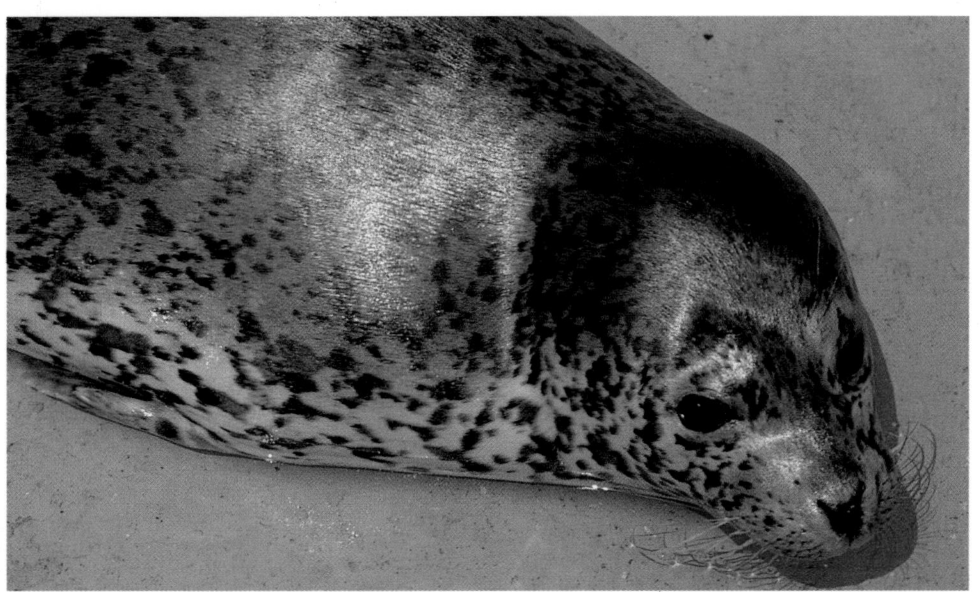

This harp seal and her pup (far left) are nearly helpless when out of the water, only able to move at a snail's pace. Female spotted seals (left) have mystified scientists for their ability to locate their young on floating ice packs.

arrives, they head north with the melting ice; during the short summer months, they are very common along the northern Arctic shores.

Like many Arctic mammals, spotted seals employ unusual breeding strategies to help ensure their young's survival. Each spring, the seals pair up, forming a monogamous relationship that lasts at least through the breeding season. Mating generally occurs in April or May, but the fertilized egg is not implanted in the uterus for several months after that, giving the seal an unusually long gestation period of ten months or more. The baby seal is finally born the following March, having missed the bitter winter that probably would have killed it. Remarkably, by the time it gives birth, the mother spotted seal will be living alone; the baby seal's father is long gone. Six weeks later, as the young seal is being weaned, the mother will once again pair up, probably with a new male.

Because the spotted seal is a solitary breeder, unlike the harbor seal and other species which live in colonies, it poses another fascinating mystery, perhaps the hardest of all to solve. The spotted seal spends most of its time on the fringes of the Arctic ice cap and chooses to raise its young on

A female harp seal, with its jaws agape (far right), casts a threatening glance at an intruder. The ringed seal (right) is favorite prey for the polar bear.

© Carleton Ray/The National Audubon Society Collection/PR

a slab of floating ice that may be only 3 yards (3 meters) long. This tiny ice island, separated both from the mainland and from larger expanses of pack ice, gives the defenseless pup protection from bears, wolves, and other predators. But it also drifts with the current, as much as 1 mile (1.6 kilometers) or more each day. After the mother seal dives in search of food, spending several minutes below the surface, she must be able to locate her pup on a single slab of ice among hundreds of others—a slab that will no longer be in the same position as it was when she left it.

Scientists have no concrete idea how mother spotted seals keep track of their drifting pups. Perhaps she has some kind of innate radar that charts the ocean currents and helps her deduce the ultimate location of her pup's ice island. Or perhaps she can identify some kind of unique odor produced by her young. No one knows for sure.

How the spotted seal locates food on the ocean floor is another unsolved puzzle facing marine biologists. The crabs, shrimp, and other creatures these seals crave are a quarter of a mile (two-fifths of a kilometer) below the surface in pitch-black waters. Yet the seals are able to find the food and return to their pups quickly, a seemingly amazing feat.

© Steven C. Kaufman

At first glance, the walrus looks like the world's most unlikely animal (above and center). But its great size, thick blubber, and long tusks are all-important adaptations to life in the icy water of the Arctic.

© Rod Allin/Tom Stack & Assoc.

© Mark Newman/Tom Stack & Assoc.

A harp seal pup basks in the Arctic sun (above). The harp seal is named for the horseshoe-shaped dark pattern on the back of the male.

An equally solitary but far more sedentary relative of the spotted seal is the *ringed seal*. Weighing 100 to 150 pounds (45 to 68 kilograms), the ringed seal is the smallest Arctic pinniped. Although some ringed seals breed on drifting pack ice, most choose to raise their young atop the thick ice that spreads out each winter from the mainland. Because this ice cap may extend for great distances out into the ocean during the coldest months of the year, the ringed seal has become a master builder of the breathing hole.

In the fall, as the ice cap is just forming, the ringed seal carves one or more holes through the ice to the open water below. These holes, just large enough for the seal to fit through, would quickly freeze over if not kept clear, so the seal tends them carefully throughout the winter. Without these breathing holes, the seal would have no access to the shrimp, crabs, and fish that make up its diet—but the holes also create great dangers for the seal. As described in chapter three, polar bears often stake out a ringed seal's breathing hole, swatting at the unsuspecting seal when it surfaces or stalking the unlucky pinniped as it rests on the ice. Most seals survive, but those that

© Steven C. Kaufman

Although walruses are usually peaceable creatures, bulls will occasionally battle for dominance in the herd. In these fights, both may inflict terrible wounds, but only the loser slinks away in disgrace.

don't make up a large part of the polar bear's winter diet.

Perhaps the most familiar and most beloved pinniped of all is the huge walrus, probably because its bristly face seems to have nearly human qualities. With its expansive jowls, luxurious whiskers, and button eyes, the walrus resembles someone's elderly, slightly dotty uncle. But it, too, has evolved to possess a fascinating set of survival techniques that enable this enormous mammal to thrive in the cold waters of the Far North.

Walruses are by far the largest pinnipeds found in the Arctic. Females can reach 1 ton (0.907 metric tons) in weight, while a stout bull can exceed 2 tons (1.8 metric tons) and measure 12 feet (3.6 meters) long. No matter what its size, however, the walrus's skin seems to have been designed for a slightly larger animal. Saggy, wrinkled, and covered with creases, the walrus's coat contributes to its comical, almost humanlike appearance.

Most walruses eat shrimp, crabs, marine worms, and other small creatures, although their favorite food is clams. You might think the walrus uses its large tusks to dig up clams from the seabed, but this is not the case. In-

Walruses are social beasts that seemingly depend on nearly constant physical contact (left). Only rarely will one—usually a young male—be seen alone (above).

stead, the walrus uses its strong lips and tongue to grab the clams' siphons and feet sticking up from the mud on the seafloor; Only these parts of the clam make it down to its stomach.

Not all walruses depend on shellfish for their diet. A population may have one or two "rogues"—individuals who have developed a taste for seal flesh. It seems that a walrus that has stumbled upon (and tasted) a dead seal may become a habitual hunter of seals and even—some experts say—of humans, hurling its massive body onto Eskimo skiffs and attacking the unlucky occupants. Rogue walruses can be easily recognized by the ingrained grease stains on their normally white tusks.

In the fall and winter months, all walruses move south of the Arctic Circle, choosing to winter along the southern fringes of the expanding ice pack. When spring arrives, the entire population moves northward in a tight group. Throughout the year, the walrus lives in herds; like many gregarious animals, this enormous mammal has developed an intricate, complex, and unique social structure that is still not completely understood by humans.

The herd itself is the focus of one such structure, with males struggling to establish dominance. The larger and fatter a bull is, and the longer his tusks, the greater the dominance he will usually attain. While these size differences often eliminate the need for actual fighting, sometimes a slightly smaller bull just won't take the hint. Then a clash does result, with the two males roaring and slashing at each other with their great tusks. Bulls with long, ugly scars are a common sight, but few if any die as a result of these clashes.

© John Warden

A walrus' tusks most often are used like a mountain-climber's pickaxe; the walrus chops a hole in the pack ice with them and pulls itself out of the water.

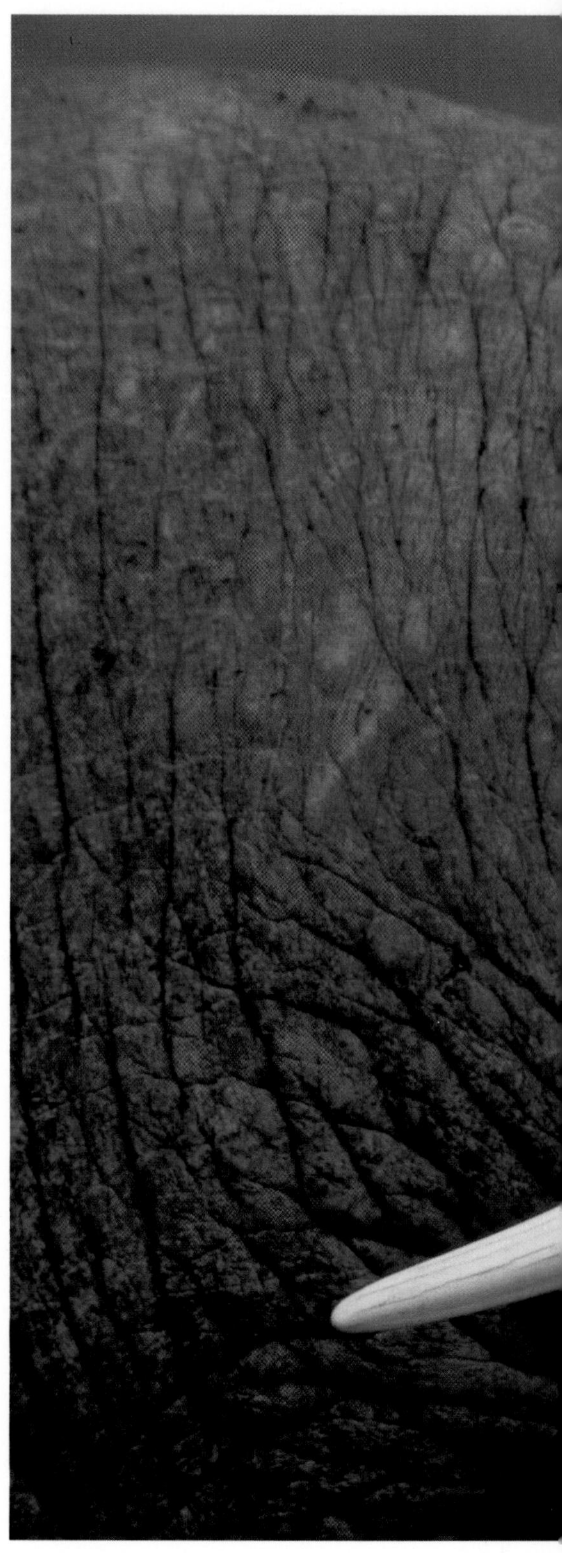

Female walruses also have tusks, although theirs are significantly thinner and shorter than those of most of the males. Although a social hierarchy also exists among walrus cows, they don't seem to employ their tusks as weapons. Instead, they, as well as the males, use these odd, elongated teeth as an aid to climbing onto the ice from the water, chopping a tusk-hold and pulling themselves up.

Walruses may live to the age of thirty or beyond and may not breed until they are ten years or older. The remarkably extended breeding period begins in January or February, when the animals congregate at the southernmost portion of their territory. At this time males and females mate, although the fetus does not begin to develop for four months. After development begins, the cow carries the baby for about another nine months.

When the young are born, in May or June of the year following their conception, the herd is in the midst of its northward migration. Weighing only about 100 pounds (45 kilograms) at birth, a pup is weak and vulnerable, although in an emergency it can swim almost immediately. Normally,

© John Warden

the baby spends most of its time resting on the ice and nursing, consuming the cow's rich milk in great quantities.

Young walruses grow slowly and remain with their mothers for two or more years. When the offspring goes off on its own (to become a small, submissive member of the herd), the female is ready to breed again, and the whole routine starts anew.

While seals and walruses depend on the water for food but breed on land or ice, another group of Arctic mammals, the *whales*, found a way to forsake the land entirely. Although fewer types of whales are found in the Arctic than elsewhere in the world's oceans, those that haunt the icy northern waters are some of the most mysterious and beautiful of all.

CHAPTER FIVE

WHALES: DENIZENS OF ARCTIC SEAS

© Robert & Linda Mitchell

© Jeff Foott

Undoubtedly the whale with the worst reputation, the orca (left) is indeed a tireless, efficient hunter. Larger whales, like this gray whale (above), often are host to numerous barnacles.

Whales are the largest mammals ever to live on earth. They have enormous brains and complex courtship rituals and some species "sing" songs of haunting beauty. They may possess great intelligence—but if they do, it is an intelligence remote from ours. Almost from the dawn of ocean exploration, and even as we decimated them through uncontrolled whaling, we have recorded the awe, fear, and fascination that the great whales provoke in us. Today, scientists continue to study whales throughout the world, but there is still much for us to learn about these huge, mysterious creatures.

We know even less about the whales that frequent the waters of the Arctic than we do about such familiar, more southerly species as the *humpback*. Perhaps the oddest and least studied of all is the *bowhead whale*, an extremely rare whale found exclusively in the cold northern waters of the Arctic.

The bowhead is a medium-sized whale that reaches a length of 50 to 60 feet (15.2 to 18.2 meters) and a weight of perhaps 60 tons (54.5 metric tons). Mostly black or gray, the bowhead has a curved jaw resembling a drawn archer's bow

(hence its name), and a contrasting white area on its lower jaw. In addition, the bowhead has no dorsal fin, giving it a plain, unusually streamlined appearance.

The bowhead whale's head seems to have evolved for a life in which ice is a common barrier to the air. The whale's nostrils are placed on an odd projection very high atop the skull. This projection, along with the whale's extraordinarily thick and large skull, allows the bowhead to batter its way through ice more than a foot (30.5 centimeters) thick. Once it has created a small crack in the ice, its strangely situated nostrils can reach the air, even if the rest of the whale can't.

Bowheads are *baleen whales*, which means that instead of teeth they possess great, fringed plates (baleen, or *whalebone*) that act as sieves to filter the water for food. This food consists of small creatures—including shrimp, worms, and baby crabs—that

© National Marine Mammal Lab

The bowhead, so named for the way it uses its bow-shaped head to break through the ice, is the most common Arctic whale.

are collectively called *krill*. Each whale must eat more than a ton of krill each day, which indicates how abundant krill must be in the bowhead's range.

Historically, bowheads have been a prize catch for the native Arctic people, who depended on the whale's meat and blubber for food. Despite this hunting, the bowhead was once relatively common in the Arctic's waters—but that was before large-scale commercial whaling began in the mid-nineteenth century. For more than fifty years after professional whalers "discovered" this northern whale, they killed hundreds each year, harvesting oil for use as lamp oil and baleen that ended up as corset stays. By 1935, when the bowhead was finally protected, the whale was nearly extinct.

Even today, the bowhead population has not recovered. Only several dozen are killed each year by the Eskimo, who retain the right to hunt them under strictly controlled conditions. Even with these controls, only 2,500 of them survive in Arctic waters. Scientists believe that the bowhead population may have been so reduced that the species will never

© Walt Anderson

escape the shadow of extinction.

A far more familiar baleen whale—one of the best known in North America, in fact—has a similar story, but one with a happier ending. This is the 15 to 35-ton (13.6 to 21.7 metric tons) *gray whale*, a mottled, slender, 40 to 50-foot (12.2 to 15.2-meter) species that traverses nearly the entire Pacific coast from Mexico to the United States to Canada each year. As a result of this migration, millions of people along this coastline get a close-up look at gray whales each year, even from the shore.

The gray whale's annual 6,000-mile (9,654-kilometer) migration each way is one of the longest of any mammal's, closely resembling that of many Arctic-dwelling birds. Winters are spent in tropical Baja, California, where the whales rest, court, and mate in calm, warm-water lagoons. Oddly, scientists believe that the gray whales fast at these wintering grounds, losing up to a quarter of their weight in the months that pass between meals.

In late February or early March, the whales—including the newly pregnant females—leave the warm lagoons and begin the slow journey north. Not until June do they reach their summering grounds in the

© Robert & Linda Mitchell

The gray whale undertakes one of the longest annual migrations of any whale, journeying from far northern waters to warm lagoons off the coast of Mexico. Calves born in these lagoons must make the 6,000-mile (9,654-kilometer) journey within two months of birth.

Bering, Chukchi, and Beaufort seas of the North Pacific and Arctic Oceans. Here, at last, they eat, feasting on the vast quantities of bottom-dwelling creatures that are found here and regaining the weight they've lost during their long migration.

In September or October, their southward journey begins, as the population—including the significantly more pregnant females—heads back toward Baja, California. Here, early the following year, the calves are born, a little more than a year after they were conceived. Within two months, however, they must accom-

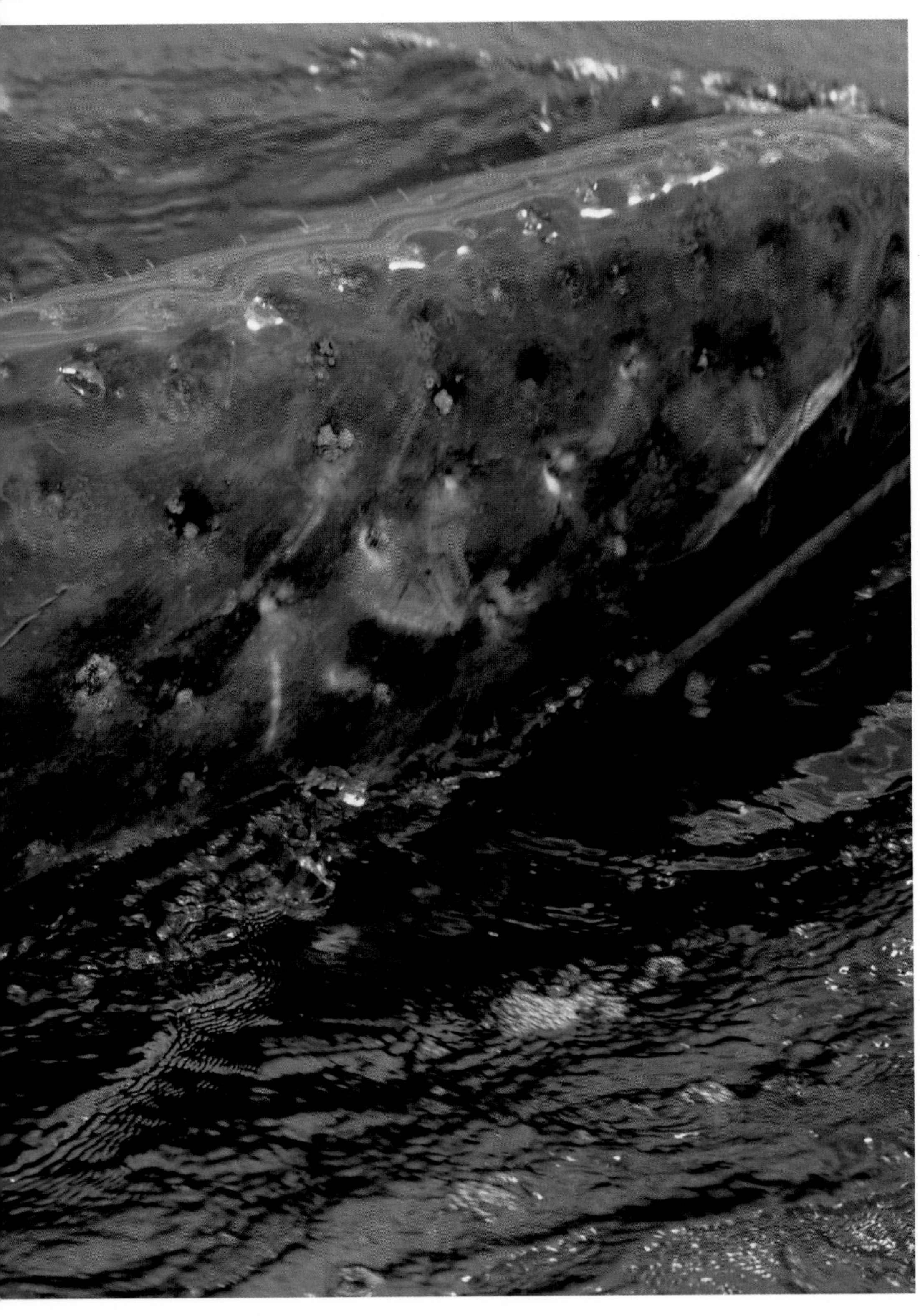

pany their elders on the northward journey. Six or seven years (and migrations) later, they, too, will mate, although they will not reach full size until they are past their thirtieth year. Overall, gray whales may live to be seventy years old, although most don't reach such a venerable age.

Before the mid-nineteenth century, hundreds of thousands of gray whales swam off the western coast of North America—but that was before the professional whalers found them. Despite the fact that they produced an oil far poorer in quality than some other whale species, the grays were so easy to find and kill (particularly in their shallow southern wintering grounds) that whalers slaughtered them at a breathtaking rate. As a result, by the turn of this century, the gray whale, like the bowhead, was on the verge of extinction.

A slump in the demand for whale oil and baleen kept the species alive until

Professional whalers brought the gray whale close to extinction a century ago. Now, though, the species is fully protected—and young gray whales like this one are helping guarantee that the species will survive.

© William Froelich/Envision

When whales sound (dive), they leave a distinctive "footprint," a smooth patch of water that remains visible for a surprisingly long time (above).

Both the beluga (right) and the orca (far right) are toothed whales. But while the beluga eats mostly fish, the orca may hunt and kill even the great blue whale.

© Jeff Foott

© Steven C. Kaufman

© Jeff Foott

The handsome beluga (above) is one of the most common Arctic whales, traveling in noisy pools in icy bays and rivers. The orca (right) is a great wanderer, journeying to wherever seals, squid, dolphins, or other prey is most abundant.

1937, when the gray whale was granted full protection by the United States, with equal protection soon following from Mexico and Canada. Even so, the population has grown very slowly since most fertile females produce only one calf every two to three years. Today, somewhere between ten and fifteen thousand survive—but at least these are in no current danger of extinction.

Several other baleen whales, including the 30-foot (15.2-meter) *minke whale* and the enormous, 80-foot (24.3-meter) *fin whale*, live in Arctic waters, while still others (including the magnificent *great blue whale*, which can grow to a length of 100 feet [30.5 meters] and weigh 200 tons [181 metric tons]) inhabit waters not far south of the Arctic Circle. However, the only other true Arctic-dwelling *cetaceans*—aquatic mammals, including whales, dolphins, and porpoises—are toothed whales, far smaller than their krill-eating kin.

Three toothed whales are particularly representative of the Arctic seas. One, the unicornlike *narwhal*, is among the strangest and least studied of all whales. The second, the *beluga*, or *white whale*, is a striking inhabitant of coastal bays and rivers. And the third is perhaps the most famous and

misunderstood whale of all: the *orca*, or *killer whale*.

There are a good many reasons why narwhal are so little known. They inhabit only the coldest, murkiest waters of the Far North, close to the North Pole itself. They are small (no more than 15 feet [4.6 meters] long) and hard to find, since they are constantly wandering across their frigid territory. Thus, much of our current knowledge of the narwhal comes from the analysis of dead individuals that have washed ashore, not an ideal way of learning about the life history of any animal.

We do know that narwhals have only two teeth—but what spectacular teeth they can be. While in the female these teeth normally remain within the mouth, male narwhals always grow at least one tusk, which can be 8 feet (2.4 meters) in length. This sharp, slender tusk resembles a screw with a leftward thread. Sometimes a narwhal will sport a second tusk opposite the first. This is especially odd, since the narwhal's second tusk also has a leftward spiral, while in most animals, each side of the body is an exact reverse image of the other.

Scientists have long argued over the tusk's use. It can't be important in finding food, as tuskless females survive quite happily. Apparently, the male's tusk is actually a secondary sexual characteristic, used in attracting females and in jousting with other males for dominance. In this way, it most resembles the antlers of a deer, which are put to a similar use.

Beluga whales and their habits are far better understood by scientists because the whale itself is so much tamer and more accessible than most other whales. An even, chalky white, these 15-foot (4.5-meter) whales are also the only ones to adapt easily to captivity, making them popular exhibits at many large aquariums.

Though belugas born in captivity rarely survive, they are easily tamed from the wild and readily adapt to life in an aquarium.

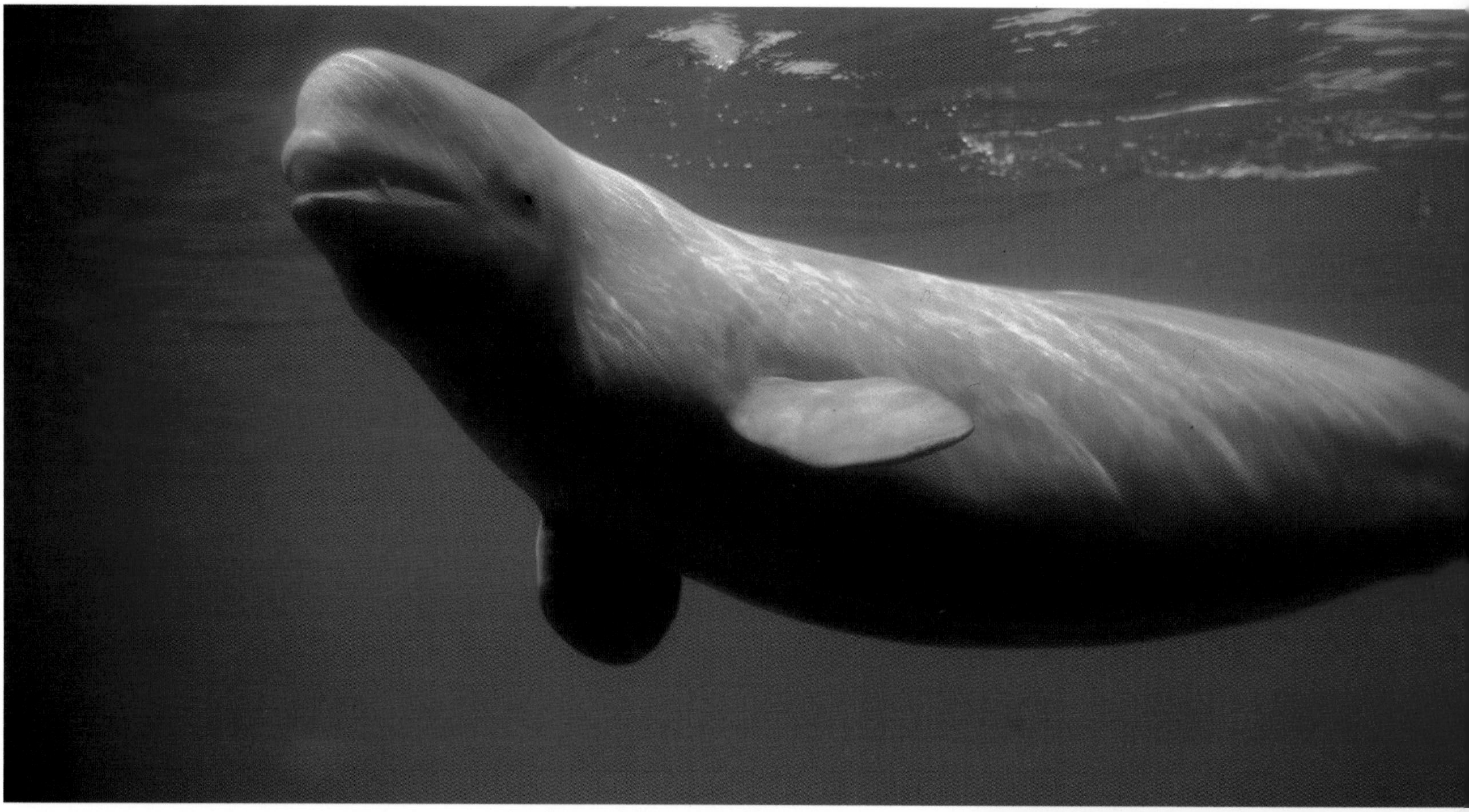

© Jeff Foott

Belugas (above) and orcas (right) are both toothed whales, but the white whale will always give its black-and-white relative a wide berth. No marine animal can withstand a determined attack from an orca pack.

Belugas are found in both Arctic and subpolar waters. They are among the most sociable of whales, with groups (called pods) sometimes numbering in the hundreds. Communication between members of the herd consists of grunts and moos loud enough to be heard from shore.

Although belugas have never been hunted commercially, they are an important source of food, blubber, and oil to the Eskimo inhabitants of coastal Arctic villages, who continue to hunt them today. A far greater threat to the species came recently, when commercial fishermen showed that belugas were decimating the salmon population of Bristol Bay in Alaska. The whales were actually journeying upriver in spring to feast on the baby salmon, thereby threatening the local fishing industry.

Many of the fishermen suggested that any beluga found eating salmon be shot. Others resisted the idea, and the battle continued—until someone came up with a brilliant suggestion. Belugas are terrified of orcas, which prey on them. So, the fishermen reasoned that if they played recordings of orca songs (beautiful, far-carrying sounds), they might chase away the belugas. And they did, helping to rescue both the baby salmon and the whales themselves.

© Jeff Foott

Streamlined, powerful, agile—the orca is ideally suited to its role as "wolf of the sea." In captivity, however, the orca is docile, easily trained, and affectionate.

Of course, many of the same people who now use orca songs to protect their livelihood would have no desire to meet the singer of them. In fact, no whale (and few animals of any kind) has a worse reputation than the "killer whale." Tabloids, horror movies, even memoirs of shipwreck survivors have painted a lurid picture of a vicious killer who hunts for enjoyment, eats its victims alive, and has an immense thirst for vengeance.

The real orca—as opposed to the scandal-sheet monster—*is* one of the most powerful predators on earth. These black-and-white whales can reach a length of 25 to 30 feet (7.6 to 9.1 meters), and a weight of 10 tons (9 metric tons), and are easily recognized at a distance by their remarkably long dorsal fins, which may stick up 6 feet (1.8 meters) from the surface. They almost always travel in pods ranging from three or four to thirty or more; a solitary whale may have been ejected from a pod because of illness or age.

Orcas are extremely strong swimmers, sometimes achieving speeds of more than 25 knots. They use their speed and numbers to attack far larger whales, pursuing their prey until it tires, then circling and biting it until it dies. More often, orcas prey on seals and sea lions, dolphins, and fish.

Without a doubt, they are formidable hunters. But are they the implacable killers of so much overheated prose and celluloid? The answer to this question, say the experts, is easy: No. In fact, orcas are easy to tame, as anyone who has ever attended an aquarium whale-and-dolphin show can attest. These whales are gentle and intelligent. As they hunt for prey in the cold waters of the Arctic, they are simply following their natural instincts.

CHAPTER SIX

BIRDS: LIFE ON A TREELESS TUNDRA

In many ways, the hurdles that birds must overcome to live in the Arctic are as great as those confronting all the other living creatures there. They must face brutal weather, a sporadic food supply, and other conditions that temperate birds could never survive. Yet, despite their harsh environment, more than one hundred species of birds—ranging from the comical horned *puffin* to the sleek, predatory *gyrfalcon*—breed in the Arctic. While plants may have evolved more complicated survival techniques (no birds, for example, have "antifreeze" running through their veins), the birds that breed in the Far North are masters at adapting to the harsh environment.

Not all birds that breed in the Arctic face the challenges in the same way. Perhaps most importantly, only a few species live in the Arctic all year long; the rest migrate south at the first sign of fall and return, harbingers of spring, perhaps eight months later.

Resident Arctic birds, needless to say, face the greatest challenges as they weather the region's dark, barren winter. One of the best-known year-round residents is the *snowy owl*, whose white plumage is adorned with black spots and bars. (Snowy owls

© Ted Levin

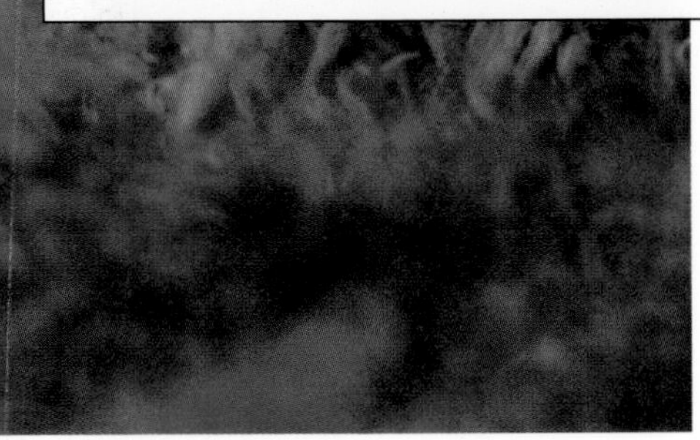

© Ted Levin

The golden plover, shown here in its stunning breeding plumage (left), spends only the Arctic summer in the Far North. This red-shouldered phalarope chick (above), barely an hour old, can already walk—a crucial benefit in its dangerous tundra home.

living farthest north are lightest; juveniles living all over the Arctic are the most heavily spotted.) Heavily feathered from beak to toe (even its feet are feathered), the snowy owl is clearly able to keep itself warm in even the most unforgiving conditions.

Found throughout nearly the entire Arctic, the snowy owl is particularly common on the tundra. Life in this treeless habitat has forced the owl to adapt in ways that make it differ from nearly every other owl on earth. For example, most owls spend their lives perched in trees, but the snowy owl chooses hills—or, more recently, buildings—as vantage points. Also, nearly all owls are nocturnal; the snowy owl, however, hunts mainly during the day, scanning the bright-white tundra in search of food and then swooping silently down.

Snowy owls, like most northern birds, undergo periodic population booms when hares and lemmings,

© John Warden

The snowy owl's thick, fluffy feathers (right) provide insulation from the cold, while its mostly white plumage is perfect camouflage against the snowy tundra. The dapper Sabine's gull (far right), like many Arctic birds, finds its food in the fish-filled Arctic seas.

© Albert Kuhnigk/First Light

their natural prey, are particularly abundant. When this happens, there simply isn't enough room on the tundra for such a large owl population; in winter months, when food begins to become scarcer, large numbers of snowy owls (usually the darker juveniles) journey far south of the Arctic in search of food. They often show up along the eastern coast of the United States, for example, where they can be spotted perched on sand dunes—the closest thing to their hilly tundra homes.

While small mammals make up much of the snowy owl's diet, the owls aren't adverse to eating other birds. In the Far North, their most popular avian prey is the odd and beautiful *rock ptarmigan*. This game bird is one of the most common birds of the high tundra. It is also among the most distinctive, for the ptarmigan is one of the few birds to change color almost completely from season to season.

Both the rock ptarmigan (below) and the white-tailed ptarmigan (left) change with the Arctic seasons. During the icy winter, they sport immaculate white coats, but in summer their cryptic brown plumage blends in with the dry tundra grassland.

© Brian Milne/First Light

The reasons for these color changes are easy to understand. During the winter, when their home turf lies buried under a deep layer of snow, rock ptarmigans turn a brilliant white. Only a black tail and the male's black line through the eye (a feature that may have evolved to diffuse snow glare) interrupts their pure plumage. In summer, however, the female turns a drab, barred brown—all the better camouflage against the rocky tundra once the snow has melted. The male, a richer brown and white, helps the female raise the young by standing guard near the nest, which is always built on the ground. In any plumage, the rock ptarmigan, with its deep, gravelly voice, is a familiar sight and sound in the Arctic.

It is also the prey of perhaps the most spectacular of all northern birds: the streamlined gyrfalcon, largest of all falcons. With its wingspan of more than 4 feet (1.2 meters), this powerful predator flies with deceptively slow wing beats, yet it can be ferociously fast. Unfortunately, the laws protecting this uncommon species have not prevented poachers from smuggling many to some Middle Eastern countries where falconing still remains a popular sport.

Individual gyrfalcons can be gray, pure white, or black. All belong to the same species; white birds are most common in the northernmost, snowiest parts of the species' range, while darker birds live further south.

A bird of far less mystery than the regal gyrfalcon and of less power than the snowy owl, the glossy-black *raven* is one of the most common and best adapted birds of the Far North. This relative of the common crow can live quite happily in environments

which range from the high Arctic to temperate deserts.

Ravens, like crows, may simply be too smart for their role in life. Because they are omnivorous, they are able to find food more easily than any other Arctic-dwelling bird. During the spring and summer, they often nest on cliffs also populated by nesting seabirds, whose eggs and chicks they steal and eat. In winter months, when the seabirds have flown south, the raven will eat seeds, pick through the droppings of caribou and other large animals, and raid the carcasses of Arctic creatures that have died.

However, these large birds, with their piercing black eyes and thick, ridged beaks, don't work any harder than they have to in their search for food. Wherever people have populated the Arctic, ravens can be found happily using the local garbage dump as a buffet. This leaves the raven with plenty of time to laze around, let loose its loud, raucous call, and steal small tools and other valuables from Arctic settlements.

While the raven, gyrfalcon, and a few other species can survive in the Arctic year-round, dozens of other species use the Far North as a summer home and breeding site. Only a few of these are songbirds (that is, the warblers, thrushes, and other species so well represented in warmer regions); of those that do brave the short Arctic summer, perhaps the most commonly seen and widespread is the *snow bunting.*

With its flashy black-and-white plumage and jerky, shimmering flight, the snow bunting ventures further north in summer than any other songbird. Flocks have been spotted far above the Arctic Circle, near the North Pole itself, but the species is more commonly seen on the tundra and further south.

The snow bunting has evolved several unusual strategies for surviving in the Far North. Unlike most songbirds, which nest in trees, the snow bunting utilizes hills, small cliffs, and other areas to provide protection and camouflage for its eggs and young. In addition, while a single glance at the bunting's short, conical beak confirms that it is adapted for seed eating, the species actually depends on insects for a large part of its summer diet in the largely seedless Arctic.

In fall, the snow bunting flees the Arctic cold and migrates to more southerly parts of Europe, Asia, and North America.

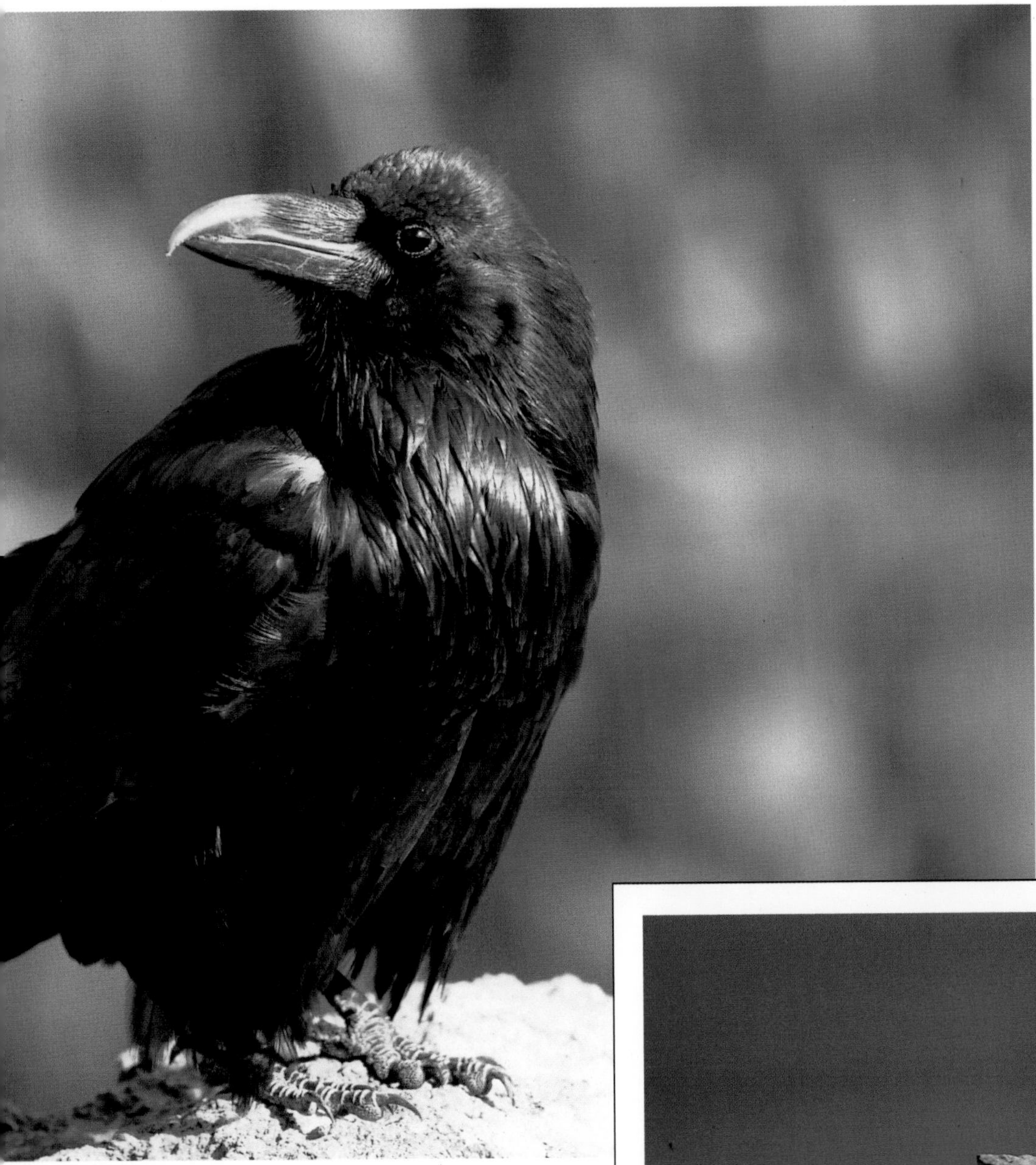

© Leonard Lee Rue III/Tom Stack & Assoc.

The world's northernmost songbird, the snow bunting (below), like most other Arctic species, migrates far south during the long northern winter. The raven (left) stays all winter, eating everything from insects to garbage.

© Brian Milne/First Light

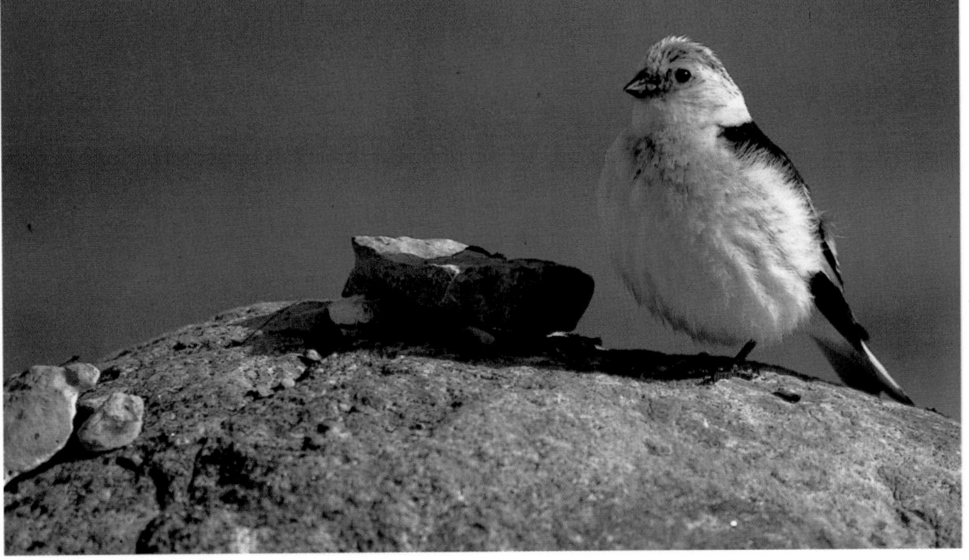

© John W. Warden

© Steven C. Kaufman

The tundra swan (center), one of the most familiar Arctic birds, is found on large ponds and lakes throughout the North American tundra. The Pacific loon (left) is noted for its haunting, eerie cry. The long-tailed jaeger (below right) is often found near nesting sea-bird colonies where it attacks young birds and scavenges carrion.

Perhaps the most remarkable journey of any bird on earth, however, is undertaken each year by another northern nester: the *arctic tern*, a small seabird.

During the summer, this tern, adorned with a natty black cap and red bill and legs, chooses to nest on sandy Arctic beaches and riverbanks, scraping a small depression into which it lays its eggs. Come fall, the Arctic tern feels the call of the warm south. Unlike most other migrants, however, it does not head to southern Canada or Europe or to the welcoming shores of the United States.

Instead, for unclear reasons, every Arctic tern heads past the temperate regions, past the tropics of southern Asia and South America, past the towering Andes Mountains and the frigid wastes of the Patagonia region of South America—all the way to the Antarctic ice cap. This small bird flies more than 10,000 miles (16,090 kilometers) every fall and winters on frozen islands and drifting icebergs, only to return to the Arctic the following spring. The 20,000-mile (32,180-kilometer) round-trip (in some cases, the terns may actually migrate as much as 25,000 miles [40,225 kilometers]) is thought to be the longest migration of any bird. It is also one of

Unlike most songbirds, the snow bunting (left) nests in crags and small caves where it can protect itself from predators. The Arctic tern (below) breeds in the Far North, but migrates an astounding 10,000 miles (16,090 kilometers) to the Antarctic every fall. Here, a mother feeds its day-old young.

Puffins, like this one feeding on herring, and other sea birds nest in large colonies on rocky cliffs by the sea. They may fly for miles each day in search of fish.

the most remarkable accomplishments of any member of the animal kingdom.

Another family of birds doesn't migrate anywhere near this distance. It can't boast the gyrfalcon's streamlined power or the raven's casual adaptability. Yet the Arctic's *Alcidae*—a family of fish-eating seabirds that includes such odd birds as puffins, murres, and *razorbills*—are among the Far North's most well known and distinctive creatures. The reason is simple: Many members of this family, known as *alcids*, breed in vast colonies on seaside or offshore cliffs, in a spectacle that is nearly unsurpassed in the world of birds.

The numbers of alcids found in these colonies can be overwhelming. According to biologist Tony Gaston of the Canadian Wildlife Service, perhaps three and a half million thick-billed murres can be found in the eastern portion of the Canadian Arctic. Nearby, in the Thule district of Greenland's Baffin Bay, somewhere between 10 and 20 million *dovekies* (a small, pigeonlike alcid) nest, resulting in more birds in one place than can be found anywhere else in the Northern Hemisphere.

Why is it that most birds nest individually or in small groups, while some, like the alcids, gather in nearly uncountable numbers on seemingly unforgiving and barren cliffs? To find the answer, Gaston and other scientists had to unlock the mysteries of alcid population dynamics.

First, when murres, dovekies, and other alcids return to the Arctic from their southern wintering grounds, they must solve many of the same problems that other nesters in the region must face. Paramount among these is that the Far North has no trees. The alcids must nest close to their marine food sources, yet no bird has yet developed the ability to build a nest on the water itself.

© Tom J. Ulrich

Ptarmigans and other birds that nest on the treeless tundra do so solitarily, as any colony of nests would immediately capture the attention of such predators as the arctic fox and the snowy owl. Alcids, therefore, have no choice but to lay their eggs on the steep, seemingly precarious sides of the cliffs that stretch along the Arctic's coastline.

But this still did not answer some fundamental questions. Why do alcids like the thick-billed murre choose to nest colonially? And why, as Gaston noticed, did the smallest murre nesting colony in this study area contain more than ten thousand mated pairs? No behavior pattern evolves without a logical explanation; there have to be good reasons for the lack of smaller colonies. It was up to Gaston to find the reasons.

After years of studying the habits of nesting murres, Gaston has developed a theory that is both fascinating and pleasing in its simplicity. The murres, he explains, feed on a variety of small fish and shrimplike animals, many of which thrive far out at sea, a great distance from the birds' nesting cliffs. In fact, a murre seeking food for itself and its young may have to fly for two hours each way every time it needs to eat.

© Tom J. Ulrich

If this isn't difficult enough, weather, wind conditions, changing currents, and other factors may mean the overnight disappearance of some food sources and the appearance of others far away. Murres, flying to areas that were teeming with fish just a day before, may find barren waters and have to start the search again.

Gaston believes that if murres nested individually, this ongoing hunt for distant food would simply be too stressful for one bird alone. Many would die of exhaustion, dooming their unprotected young to quick starvation. And the species would quickly decline and eventually become extinct.

In a large colony, however, hundreds of individuals are searching for food at all times (twenty-four hours a day during the Arctic's nightless summer). No single murre has to cover as much territory; Gaston has noted that murres perched on the nesting cliffs watch the flight patterns of incoming birds. In this way, they quickly discover where that day's schools of fish are located and can fly directly to the site. This is a remarkably efficient and successful survival strategy for the murres. It is also a clear example of the stresses of life in the Arctic—and the brilliant methods that the area's birds use to overcome them.

Both common murres (far left) and thick-billed murres (left) are colonial nesters, laying their eggs precariously on stone cliffs. Some eggs undoubtedly are broken, but most are safe from predators unwilling to scramble down the steep rock faces.

CHAPTER SEVEN
THE ENDLESS STRUGGLE: HUMANS IN THE ARCTIC

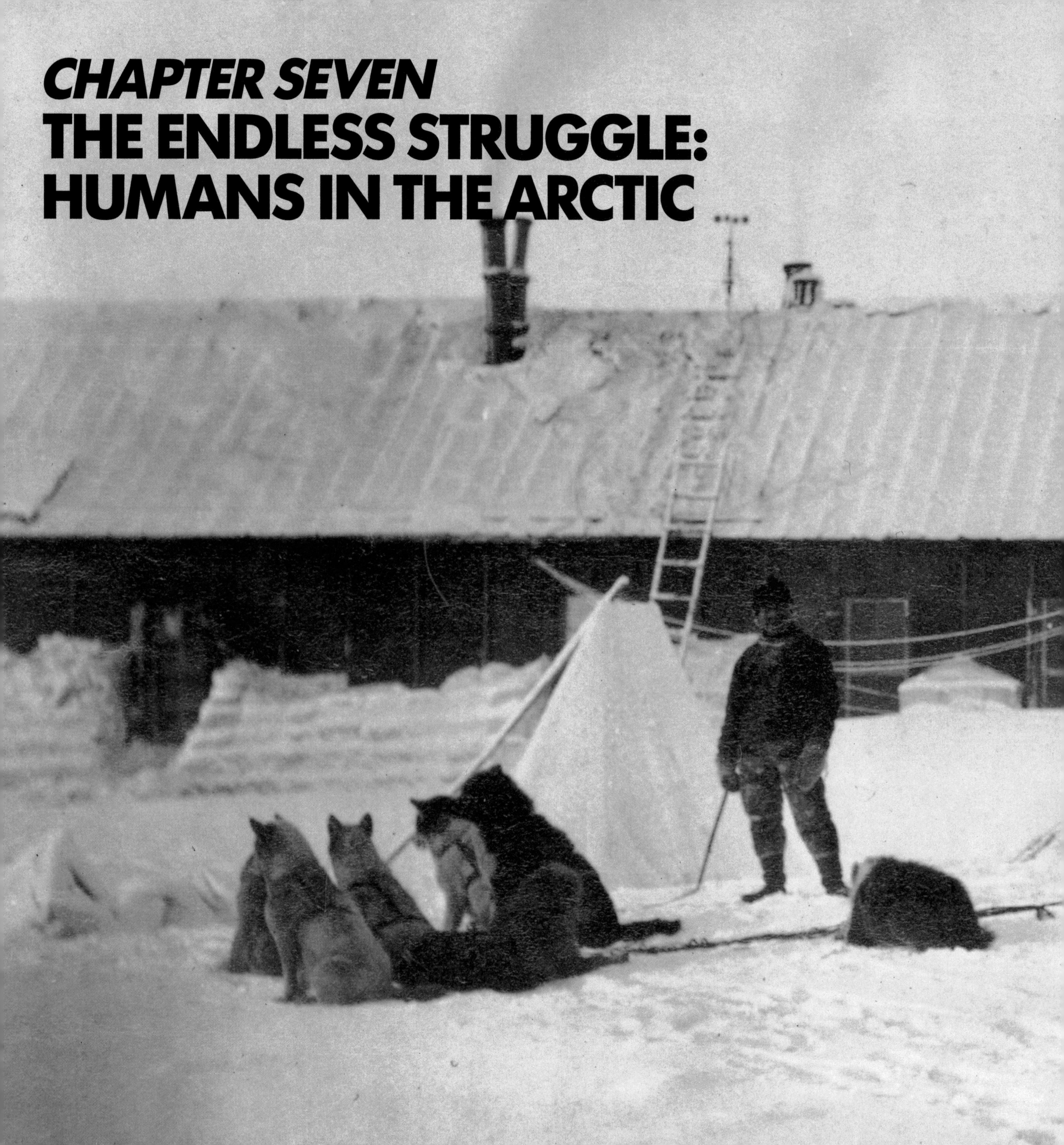

When you think of Arctic exploration, you might remember seeing a black-and-white picture of Admiral Robert Edwin Peary struggling through the bitter cold toward the North Pole. Or perhaps you might recall reading about an earlier adventurer, Sir John Franklin, who helped discover the Northwest Passage. But these two men—and the dozens of others who have achieved some fame through their attempts to map the northernmost lands and oceans—were neither the first nor the bravest of the explorers.

Nor were they the first (or last) to find out that the Arctic can be a harsh home. From the earliest primitive tribe that attempted to settle along the fringes of the ice cap, to the oil workers who must contend with unstable permafrost today, every individual who attempts to carve out a

Fur coats, heavy gloves, and waterproof boots helped keep Admiral Peary and his team of Arctic explorers alive. These important articles of clothing remain essential to northern residents today.

Library of Congress

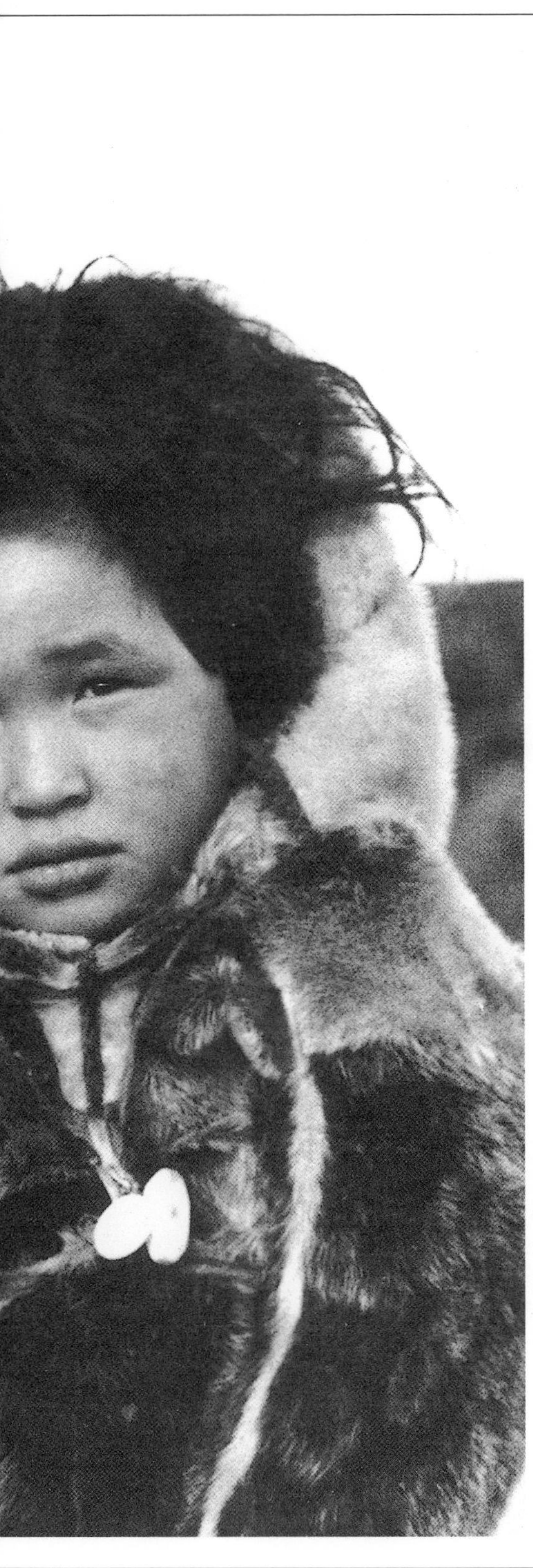

niche in the Far North rediscovers a fundamental truth: the Arctic may be the perfect habitat for the polar bear and the narwhal, but humans can only survive there if they devise ingenious strategies as complex as those of any native animal.

Experts differ on when and how the first primitive people colonized the Arctic. Many think that the first colonization of North America from Asia (and, perhaps, the Arctic regions as well) took place thirty thousand or more years ago. Others, however, set the date of North American colonization as little as twenty-three thousand years ago. Unfortunately, no one can be sure when the Artic itself harbored its first permanent settlements; the unforgiving climate and unmelting ice have long since destroyed or hidden most of the stone tools and other remnants of any ancient culture.

Most experts now believe, however, that the interior Arctic harbored a permanent colony about five thousand years ago. Some of the colonists may have come across from what is now Siberia, sailing the perilous waters in primitive boats. Others may have walked north from more southerly lands, such as the comparatively verdant expanses of what is now interior Alaska.

Some of these migrations may have occurred during one of the Arctic's occasional warmer periods, during which the ice cap receded and plants and animals became more abundant. Unfortunately, these long warm spells were always followed by renewed cold, during which many of the area's inhabitants must have starved or frozen to death. Scientists estimate that the rigors of life in the Arctic may have kept these early populations in the hundreds or low thousands for thousands of years.

Today's Eskimo peoples are directly

Native residents of the Arctic have long reaped the benefits of utilizing their environment for survival, including the seal skin parkas these Eskimos are wearing.

descended from the Thule, a culture that established itself during one of the Arctic's periodic warming trends, a time now dubbed the **climatic optimum** 900-1100 A.D. During the optimum, the numbers of marine animals off the area's coasts skyrocketed. Seals, whales, walrus—all were suddenly far more accessible.

The creative, aggressive Thule took advantage of this newfound plenty. Using sealskin boats (equipped with oars or sails), kayaks, and dogsleds, they were extremely successful hunters, and the Thule population grew rapidly. They colonized new areas of the high Arctic, built permanent villages, and established a complex, structured culture that was a remarkable achievement.

Unfortunately, even the Thule could not survive the cooling trend that followed the climatic optimum. This cold spell, which lasted for more than seven hundred years, forced the breakup of Thule society. The result

was the appearance of isolated cultures, separated by vast expanses of barren land. Even worse, the return of harsh conditions meant that the Arctic's inhabitants were once again forced to struggle for survival—a guarantee that recent cultural advances would be abandoned and new ones developed only slowly and grudgingly. The Eskimo that greeted the first European explorers were in the midst of this struggle.

No one knows for sure who was the first European to set eyes on the Arctic. Most likely, it was a Greek adventurer named Pytheas, who undertook a great journey about 325 B.C. and seems to have visited what is now either Iceland or northern Norway. Although most of his writings have been lost, it seems that Pytheas actually did sail close enough to the Arctic to spy drifting pack ice.

Nearly a thousand years passed before more concerted efforts to visit the Arctic took place, this time by the Norsemen, the most adventurous of early explorers. By the turn of the ninth century, they had begun to colonize Iceland. A century later, the famous Eric the Red established a colony called Greenland, naming that icy, barren land that way in order to induce more settlers to join him.

Whaling boats covered with seal skin (above left) are sturdy, durable vessels for Eskimos braving the frigid seas. On land, the most efficient travel available is a streamlined sled pulled by strong, nearly tireless Eskimo dogs called Kingmits (left).

© Dwight Ellefsen/Envision

© John Warden

With thoroughly insulated parkas (left) and hand-hewn tools (like this drill, right), Eskimos have adapted to the harsh challenges of their northern terrain. The advantages of modern technology and housing (above), however, have not proved as efficient as their traditional building methods.

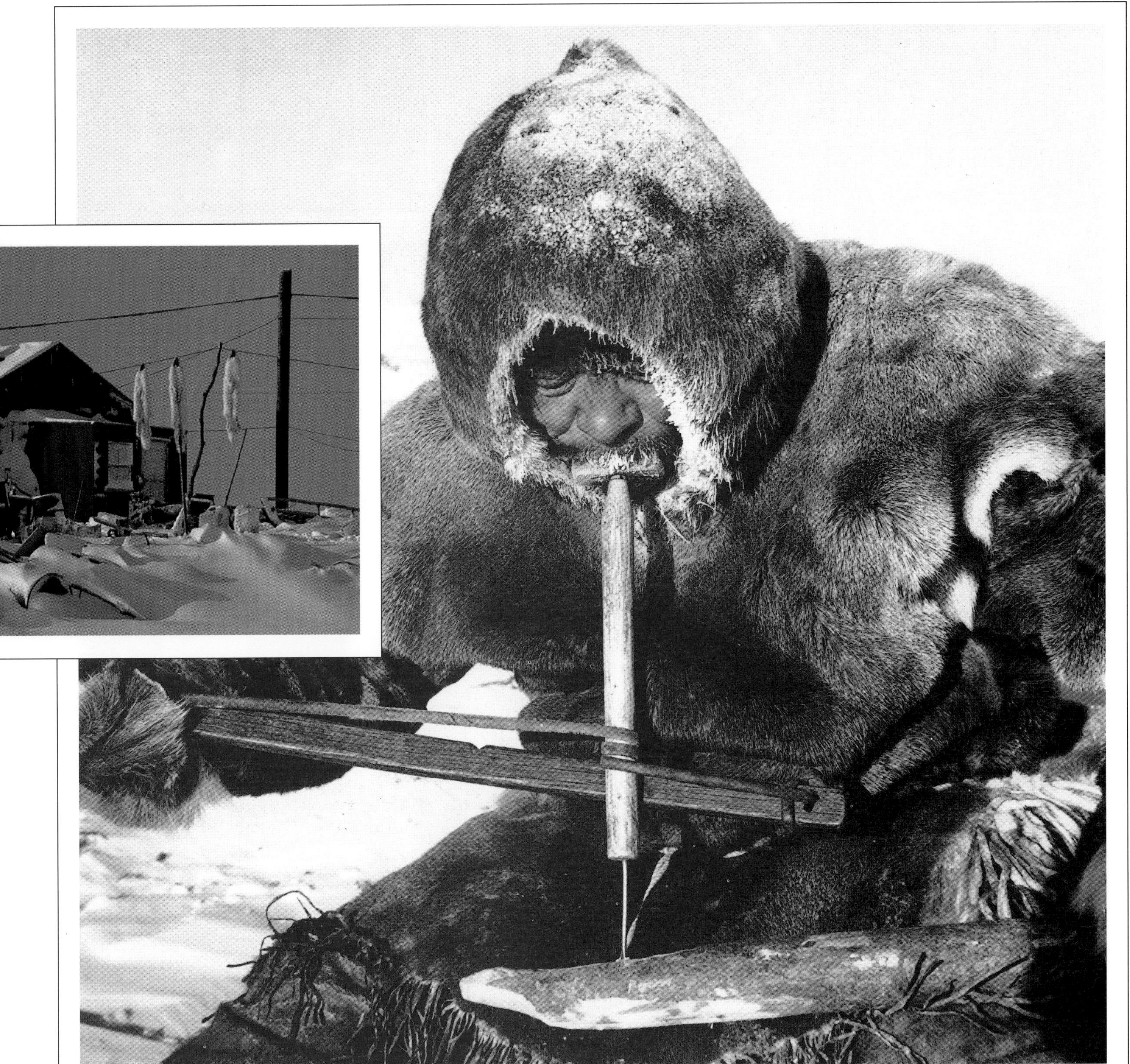

© Ted Levin

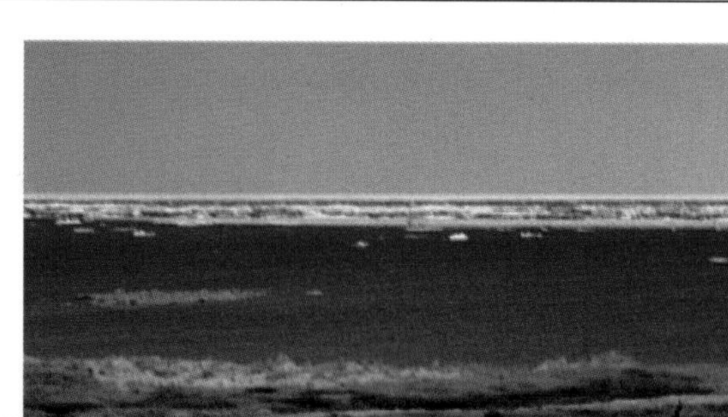

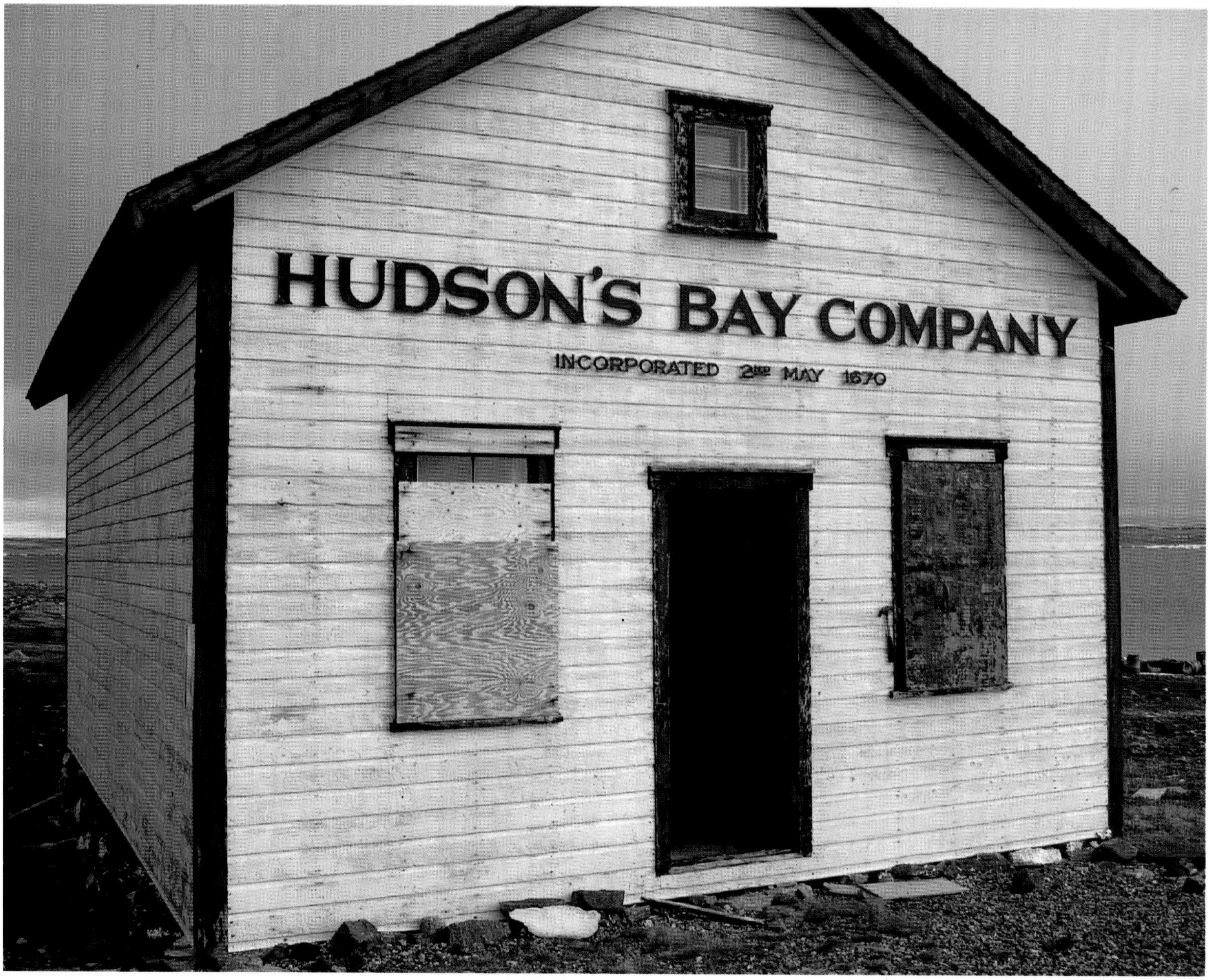

© Robert L. Harrison

Hudson Bay, viewed here from the shore of Churchill, Manitoba (left), was first discovered nearly four centuries ago. The bay area quickly became an important trapping and trading center for the Hudson's Bay Company (far left), which still exists today. The company provided a lifeline for hard-pressed tundra residents.

Once again, however, the Arctic climate had the last word. Most of the Norse colonization of Greenland took place during the years of the climatic optimum. Unfortunately, when the next cold phase began, these settlements soon disappeared. One can only begin to imagine the cruel fates they met.

Yet another centuries-long gap came and went before the intrepid British turned their attention to the exploration of the Far North. One of the first early explorers was Sir Martin Frobisher, who set out for Greenland in 1576, only to interrupt his journey to return with a shipful of what he believed was gold, but was actually worthless rock.

More successful expeditions were soon to follow. In the late sixteenth and early seventeenth centuries, Henry Hudson discovered what is now called Hudson Bay in northeastern Canada, and William Baffin mapped much of the Canadian Arctic. Others—particularly the Dutch explorer Willem Barents, who sailed far into the Arctic Ocean and died while seeking a direct passage between the Atlantic and Pacific—also helped draw a more complete picture of the North American Arctic.

The eighteenth century was the heyday of Russian exploration of the Arctic—yet that nation's most famous and successful navigator was a Dane named Vitus Bering. Between 1725 and 1741, Bering and a squadron of Russian explorers discovered Arctic islands, mapped the northern Siberian coastline, and sailed the passage that runs between Siberia and northernmost Alaska (now called the Bering Strait). Like so many other explorers of the Arctic, Bering perished of scurvy during one of his journeys in 1741.

Nineteenth-century Arctic exploration had a similarly tragic cast. Sir John Franklin of Britain set out to explore the North American Arctic Ocean in 1846, only to have his two ships quickly caught in advancing sea ice. For three years, during which many—including Franklin himself—died, the crewmen awaited rescue. Finally, the survivors made a desperate attempt to hike south. All perished in the effort.

Oddly, this aborted mission led to many major Arctic discoveries. In the massive attempt to rescue Franklin and his crew over several years, other explorers mapped vast expanses of the Arctic coastline between 1850 and 1860—far more than had ever been charted before.

Library of Congress

Until the twentieth century, Arctic exploration was a litany of disaster. Both Sir John Franklin (right) and Adolphus Greely (far right) led nineteenth-century expeditions that ended in great loss of life—including their own.

Library of Congress

The twentieth century was to dawn before a truly successful American expedition to the Arctic took place. In the late 1800s, several journeys sponsored by the United States had ended tragically; both an 1879 expedition led by naval officer George Washington De Long and an 1881 jaunt headed by the Army's Adolphus Greely met with disaster and much loss of life.

In the early 1900s, Robert Peary chose a different method in his push to be the first man to reach the North Pole. Unlike many previous explorers, who arrived in the Arctic pitifully un-

Library of Congress

prepared to face its harsh conditions, Peary was a student of Eskimo survival strategies. Dressed in Eskimo parkas, using Eskimo dogsleds, and employing Eskimo guides as his aides, Peary, his companion, Matthew Henson, and four Eskimo reached the top of the world on April 6, 1909. Many people today believe that Henson, a black man, played a far greater role in the expedition than he was ever given credit for and may actually have been the first to reach the North Pole itself. The color of his skin may have kept Henson from achieving the fame he deserved.

Today, humans have visited nearly every part of the Arctic—but we cannot be said to have conquered it. Even now, at a time when humans live year-round in the most barren regions, settlers still depend on supplies brought in from the outside world by airplane as well as on modern building materials that still cannot always withstand the rigors of the Arctic.

The Eskimo face a far more serious set of challenges than do the more recent human arrivals. In their attempt to hold onto traditional hunting and social practices yet reap the benefits of twentieth-century civilization, they must avoid the prejudice, poverty, alcoholism, and other pitfalls

Library of Congress

By adopting local dress and using native guides and dogsleds, Robert Peary (far left) and Matthew Henson (left) became the first explorers to reach the North Pole and return home alive.

The Arctic environment is a fragile one struggling to survive the increasing threat of human settlement and exploitation.

that seem to invade nearly every native population after its land has been settled by outsiders.

One of the greatest threats to the Eskimo is one that also faces the Arctic's other inhabitants—one that, in fact, imperils the Arctic itself. This, of course, is environmental destruction—the degradation of a land that seems mighty and untouchable, but is actually one of the earth's most fragile corners. Already, such traditional Eskimo food sources as the bowhead whale have been hunted by commercial whalers to the brink of extinction; if these whales do become extinct, another link will be broken between the Eskimo and their independent past. Similarly, commercial fishing industries may soon threaten populations of fish, leading to plunging populations of such marine fish eaters as seals, which many Eskimo depend on for food and clothing.

Other threats are even larger and more frightening. Air pollution from distant factories is sullying the once pristine Arctic environment; no one knows what ultimate destruction this pollution may cause. Already, it may be creating a greenhouse effect that blocks the sun's energy from escaping into the atmosphere. The resulting warming trend may begin to melt the vast Arctic ice cap, raising sea levels across the world. The potentially disastrous consequences for coastal cities—as well as for the Arctic itself—can barely be imagined.

None of these problems lend themselves to easy solutions. But luckily, the United States, Canada, the Soviet Union and the other countries that border the Arctic have already begun to work together to define and solve the threats facing the Far North. Only through a deeper understanding of the region's essential fragility and a farsighted stewardship that crosses international borders can the Arctic remain the spectacular land of the imagination it has been for so long.

© Ellen C. Sandbert/Envision

BIBLIOGRAPHY AND INDEX

BIBLIOGRAPHY

Burt, William H. and Richard P. Grossenheider, *A Field Guide to the Mammals* (Boston, Mass.: Houghton Mifflin Company, 1952).

Davids, Richard C. and Dan Guravich, *Lords of the Arctic* (New York: Macmillan Publishing Co., Inc., 1982).

Lopez, Barry, *Arctic Dreams* (New York: Charles Scribner's Sons, 1986).

____________, *Of Wolves and Men* (New York: Charles Scribner's Sons, 1978).

Lucas, Joseph and Susan Hayes, *Frontiers of Life: Animals of Mountains and Poles* (Garden City, New York: Doubleday and Company Inc., 1976).

McPhee, John, *Coming Into the Country* (New York: Farrar, Straus & Giroux, 1976).

Mowat, Farley, *Never Cry Wolf* (Boston, Mass.: Little, Brown and Co., 1963).

Reardon, Jim, ed., *Alaska Mammals* (Edmonds, Wash.: The Alaska Geographic Society, Vol. 8, No. 2, 1981).

INDEX

Page numbers in italics refer to captions and illustrations.

D

E

F

G

H

J

K

L

M

N

O

P

R

S

T

U

Yellowknife
Port Radium
Amundsen G.
Sachs Harbour
15
Coppermine
Holman I.
Banks I.
M'Clure Str.
Victoria I.
Mould Bay
Pr. Patrick I.
Melville
QUEEN
Cambridge Bay
Visc. Melville Sd.
Mackenzie King I.
Borden I.
100°
Garry L.
N. MAG. POLE
ELIZABETH
Pr. of Wales I.
Isachsen
Bathurst I.
Ellef Ringnes I.
Boothia Pen.
Somerset I.
Resolute
ISLANDS
Devon I.
Axel Heiberg I.
14
G. of Boothia
Repulse Bay
Brodeur Pen.
Lancaster Sd.
Eureka
Columbia
Peary
Byrd May
Ellesmere I.
Amundsen-
May 12,
Melville Pen.
Igloolik
Arctic Bay
Grise Fiord
Kane Basin
Alert
Anderson in
Foxe Basin
Thule
Lincoln Sea
80°
Pr. Charles I.
Pond Inlet
Dundas (Thule A.F.B.)
C. York
Hayes Pen.
C. Morris Jesup
BAFFIN BAY
Nettilling L.
Baffin I.
Melville Bay
Knud Rasmussen Ld.
Peary Ld.
Wand Sea
Clyde
Kraulshavn
Nord
13
Upernavik
King Frederik VIII Ld.
Pangnirtung
Cumberland Sd.
Davis Str.
Disko I.
Godhavn
Danmarkshavn
Holsteinsborg
GREENLAND
KALÂTDLIT-NUNÂT (Denmark)
King Christian X Ld.
Søndre Strømfjord
Shannon I.
60°
Sukkertoppen
Daneborg
NORTH AMERICA
ARCTIC OCEAN
U.S.S. Nautilus
Amundsen-Ellsworth-Nobile